colorwork
KNITTING

D1560707

25
Spectacular Sweaters, Hats, and Accessories

Sarah E. White

STACKPOLE BOOKS

For Anna, the most colorful thing I've ever made.

Published by
STACKPOLE BOOKS
5067 Ritter Road
Mechanicsburg, PA 17055
www.stackpolebooks.com

Printed in the United States of America

10 9 8 7 6 5 4 3 2 1

First edition

Cover design by Tessa J. Sweigert
Photography by:
  Tiffany Blackstone—front cover, i, 2 (center), 6, 7 (right), 8–9, 10 (top), 11–12, 13 (right), 14 (top), 15–20, 21 (bottom), 22, 25–32, 33 (top), 34, 35 (top), 36–39, 40 (right), 42–57, 62, 64–78, 81–96, 108–110
  Beth Hall—2 (top left and right), 3–5, 7 (left), 10 (bottom), 13 (left), 14 (bottom), 21 (top), 23–24, 33 (bottom), 35 (bottom), 41, 59–61, 79–80, 97–100, 102–103
  Sarah E. White—21 (middle), 40 (left), 101
  Color wheel image on pg. 1 copyright velusariot, via BigStock.com.

Library of Congress Cataloging-in-Publication Data

White, Sarah E.
  Colorwork knitting : 25 spectacular sweaters, hats, and accessories / Sarah E. White. — First edition.
      pages cm
  Includes index.
  ISBN 978-0-8117-1414-3
  1. Knitting—Patterns. 2. Color in knitting. I. Title.
  TT825.W5513 2015
  746.43'2—dc23
                              2014047392

Contents

Introduction

Many knitters are both intimidated by and enchanted with color knitting. The dramatic looks created when colors are combined with a masterful eye draw attention, but also leave some knitters with the idea that colorwork is too complex for the average knitter.

Rest assured that the techniques behind color knitting—whether basic stripes or intricate stranded knitting patterns—are not that difficult to learn. It's only a matter of focus and the amount of time involved that separate simpler projects from more complicated designs. This book will guide you through both as we explore using self-striping yarns, making stripes yourself, forming patterns with slipped stitches, stranded knitting, and intarsia while knitting a scarf, hat, a pair of mittens/gloves, a pair of socks, and a sweater with each technique.

Color knitting is a lot of fun. It's the perfect way to inject your personality into your knitting, whether through the selection of colors or the motifs and patterns you choose to use. It's also a great way to boost the skill level on basic projects, and looks impressive even though the techniques are not at all difficult.

Join me now on this color adventure!

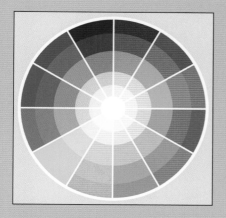

Knitting With Color

Color Basics

One of the things that makes some knitters hesitate when it comes to color knitting is not the techniques involved but the colors themselves. We don't want to pick the "wrong" colors and end up knitting something that doesn't look good or that we don't like because we end up not liking the color combination. You can always use the same colors that were called for in the pattern, but that takes some of the fun and creativity out of the process.

Being confident in your color choices comes from a combination of experience and understanding how colors work together in a design. I promise I won't get too technical, but it does help to have a vocabulary for color and how colors work together in a design.

WHAT IS COLOR?

The first thing you should know is that color is all about perception. Colors appear as they do because of how the brain processes the information the eyes give it. How we read a particular color differs depending on the amount of light in the room (and whether that light is natural or artificial) and what other colors—and the quantity of those colors—are around it. That's the fun of knitting with multiple colors in the same project: a color you might not have liked on its own can be a lot more interesting when placed next to other colors.

There are specific terms for aspects of color that can help us describe them and understand them a little better. You've probably heard these terms before: hue, saturation, and value.

The **hue** is what you're talking about when you say the name of a color that might appear on the color wheel: red, orange, or yellow-green, for example. The colors on the color wheel, you might recall from any art class you ever took, are divided into primary, secondary, and tertiary colors.

- **Primary colors:** red, yellow, blue
- **Secondary colors:** purple, orange, green
- **Tertiary colors:** red-orange, red-violet, blue-violet, blue-green, yellow-green, yellow-orange

Saturation refers to the richness of the color. Is the color pure or has white, gray, or black been added? When white is added to a pure color, that's called a *tint*. Adding gray makes a *tone*, and adding black, a *shade*. Highly saturated colors pop dramatically against other colors, while tints, tones, and shades can offer much different effects.

The **value** of a color has to do with the lightness or darkness of the color as represented on a gray scale. This is the part of color theory that always makes my head spin a little, and it may be that way for you, too. But the importance of a color's value when it comes to color knitting is that colors of different values will provide more contrast in your project, which makes it a lot more dramatic and fun.

Colorwork Techniques

Multiple colors can be incorporated in a knitted piece in a variety of ways. Some methods let the yarn do the work, while others put the control in your hands. In this book we'll be exploring five different colorwork methods on five different types of projects. I chose these techniques because they're some of my favorites, but also because they're approachable, relatively easy, and fun ways to add color to your knitting.

WORKING WITH SELF-STRIPING YARN

One of the easiest ways to inject color into your knitting is to work with a self-striping yarn. These yarns feel a little bit like magic because they're carefully dyed so they form relatively consistent stripes of color as you knit. Sometimes the color changes are dramatic, while other times they are more subtle, with blending between the colors. Either way, these yarns make it look like you used a lot of different colors of yarn when all you did was knit.

ADDING YOUR OWN STRIPES

A small step up in complexity is working projects where you add your own stripes of color. To do this, you'll have some decisions to make: How many colors will you use, and which ones? Will your stripes be horizontal or vertical? Will you choose colors for contrast or a more subtle look? Will your colors be monochromatic (all shades of blue, for example) or far apart on the color wheel? As you work through and think about the projects in the book, you'll be well equipped to answer these questions on future projects.

SLIP-STITCH PATTERNS

One of the unsung heroes of color knitting is the slip-stitch pattern. These designs can be quite dramatic but they're simple to perform because you're only working with one color on each row.

Slip-stitch patterns can be worked in two, three, or more colors. If you haven't tried this colorwork method before, now is the time to give it a try; it's a lot of fun to see the patterns develop from simply slipping stitches.

What Are Self-Patterning Yarns?

There are also some yarns—mostly sock yarns—that are billed as self-patterning yarns. These yarns are carefully plotted out to make designs that look like a stranded knitting pattern (stripes may also be involved) with no work at all on your part.

These sorts of yarns are fun to use when you're learning to knit socks, because it makes your first socks look a lot more complex than they really are. Feel free to substitute a self-patterning yarn into any of the projects that call for self-striping yarn to see what interesting patterns may emerge.

The Color-Block Striped Raglan lets you choose a few colors you love to personalize a classic sweater.

Once you choose a self-striping yarn you love, you already know you like the colors and how they play together. The Eyelet Beret takes advantage of a bright yarn to let you relax for an easy, fun knit.

Slip stitches give the Chain Stripe Hat a colorful embellishment.

Stranded knitting gives you many, many options for colorful effects!

Intarsia allows you to incorporate bold graphics like the stars on this scarf.

STRANDED KNITTING

Stranded knitting—sometimes referred to as Fair Isle, though that's one specific kind of stranded knitting—is a method that uses two colors across a row to make a pattern. Generally speaking, one color is worked for five stitches or fewer at a time and the other color is stranded loosely across the back. This makes the knit fabric extra cozy because it is double layered where the colorwork is. It's great for hats, mitts, and other garments for winter wear.

INTARSIA

Sometimes called picture knitting, intarsia is a way to make larger-scale designs on your knitting. Instead of stranding the non-working yarn across the back, you use different balls of yarn for each section of color. Yarn management is a little tricky because the strands will get tangled as you go along. But it's worth having to occasionally untangle the yarn for the fun effect of a giant flower, diamond, or other design on a sweater or hat.

Gaining Confidence in Color Choices

I will admit to not always being confident when it comes to choosing colors for a knitting project—there are so many options! But over the years I've gotten more comfortable with making color choices, both through a technical understanding of the color wheel and how colors work together and by paying attention to color in the world around me. Here are some ideas that might help you get more comfortable choosing colors for your knitting.

LOOK TO NATURE

The natural world is the best place to find wisdom about color choices. Think about the bold reds and yellows contrasting with green leaves in early fall, the gray of tree bark, the clear blue of a winter sky, delicate purple and pink in spring flowers, and the bright profusion of all sorts of hues in summer.

The more you consider the colors of nature and add them to your palette, the more confident you will be in choosing strong colors to go together in your projects.

ART AND FASHION

Artists and designers are experts at picking colors that go together well in a painting or an outfit. Look to the art and outfits you love and see if there's something about your color preferences to be learned there. Do you prefer monochromatic styles, a bold pop of color, or something more subdued? Your answers can help guide your selection of colors for your knitting projects.

JUST PLAY

One of the best ways to learn about color and what you like in your knitting projects, of course, is to experiment with yarn. Don't be afraid to go to the yarn store (where you can see the colors more accurately than buying online) and pick out a few colors of a basic wool or cotton yarn and just play with them. Use the patterns in this book or make up a pattern combining the colors and see what happens. You may not like the results you thought you would, and you may find something surprising happens with a color you didn't expect to like.

Testing Out Colors for a Project

Once you have an idea of colors you think you might like for a project, there are some things you can do to test how your proposed color choices will play together without having to knit the whole project.

First, you can try just looking at the colors next to each other in the skein or ball. Carry them around the house and look at them in different lights. Take them outside and consider them in natural light. If you like what you see, you can also take a length of each of the yarns and wind them around a ruler or a piece of cardboard in amounts somewhat relative to how they will appear in the garment (more of the main color, less of contrasting colors) to see if you have a different opinion once they're closer together.

Still happy? Next, try a swatch. Of course swatching is important for any projects you might be knitting that need to fit a body part, but it's particularly important when you're knitting colorwork because you want to see how the colors work together before you invest time in knitting the whole project.

Cast on a number of stitches that will fit at least a couple of repeats of your design for slip-stitch and stranded knitting and be at least four to six inches (10 to 15 cm) wide. Work with your desired colors through all the different motifs in the pattern, or at least four inches of a pattern if it repeats through the project.

For stripes you can do the usual four- to six-inch swatch and knit stripes in a similar fashion to the pattern you've chosen, and for intarsia you can just work a two-inch square of the contrasting color inside the main color to give you the effect of the colors together.

Make sure you bind off and wash the swatch before you make your final decision about the colors. Wool and other animal fiber yarns will bloom a bit after washing, which will make the colors look slightly different (washing can also affect gauge), and if you're using a light and dark color together you want to be sure the colors don't run.

The Leg Warmer Story

I wanted to knit some Fair Isle-inspired leg warmers, so I went to my stash and picked out a couple of colors I thought I would like. They were both kind of heathered, light greenish colors, and I thought I would like the natural look, like moss on an old stone.

I swatched my designs, and it turned out I didn't really like the combination that much. I ended up using what had originally been my main color as my background color, and I added a bright green as the main color instead. I liked this combination a lot better, even though I had thought the bright green on its own was a bit too much. (If you like the pattern, you can find it at knitting.about.com.)

A Word on Skill Level and Techniques

I didn't include suggested skill levels with the patterns because I don't want to limit newer knitters. Some of these patterns, especially the scarves, hats, and mitts, are perfect for knitters of any experience level, while tops and socks generally are better for those who've had a bit more practice. But I hope you'll give any project that strikes your fancy a try; nothing here is really that difficult.

This book assumes you know how to cast on and bind off, knit, purl, and make basic increases and decreases. Any other techniques you might need, such as picking up stitches, sewing up projects, or adding embellishments, are described in the Techniques chapter at the back of the book, beginning on page 97.

To test how colors work together, wrap pieces of yarns you are considering using together around a ruler in proportions relative to how you plan to use them in your garment.

Knitting With Self-Striping Yarns

Self-striping yarns are sneaky because they make it look like you put a lot of effort into planning stripes and changing colors while you were working, when in reality you just knit with the same yarn throughout.

These yarns are great for people who are new to color knitting because you don't have to make any color choices other than picking out a colorway you like. They also produce a garment with a dramatic, colorful effect more quickly than if you had to switch colors manually.

There are a lot fewer ends to weave in when you're finished, which means you'll literally be done quicker. But I also feel like I knit faster when working with self-striping yarn because I'm always interested in seeing what's going to happen next.

You usually see self-striping yarns used in patterns that involve stockinette stitch, because that flat knit surface allows the stripes to shine through. But it's worth experimenting with garter stitch, ribbing, and other textured stitch patterns; you may just find you like the stripes better when they're broken up a bit.

Pros of Self-Striping Yarns

- Self-striping yarns are great for new knitters and those who are new to colorwork because of their ease in color changing.
- You don't have to worry about what colors will look good together; just choose a colorway you like and knit on confidently.
- It's just like knitting with a solid-color yarn. You don't have to think about how many rows you've knit or when you need to change colors or work a pattern.
- You don't need a fancy stitch pattern; the stripes look great in stockinette and other simple stitches.

Cons of Self-Striping Yarns

- Sometimes the length of any one color is not long enough to get around your whole project. For the hat in this chapter, for instance, I used a sock yarn that does not have incredibly long repeats. Parts of the brim of the hat don't look like they were knit with self-striping yarn at all, but I like the effect. Just be aware that there is an element of chance in how the stripes may fall, and all effects may not be to your liking.
- Another thing to watch out for is that it can be difficult to find the exact same spot in the color run to start when you're knitting two similar pieces, such as two sleeves or two socks. As the designer of your piece, you decide whether this matters. On the sweater in this chapter, I decided to not let it matter, but I wanted the knee socks to match, so I worked hard to get the second sock started in the same place as the first.
- Finally, you're stuck with the colors as the yarn designer planned them, which sometimes means there's one color in a ball you don't like or wouldn't have chosen if you were plotting the stripes yourself. Of course if you wanted to cut out a color you don't like in a self-striping yarn with abrupt stripes, you could, but that takes some of the ease out of working with self-striping yarn.

How to Make a Self-Striping Project Your Own

The easiest way to change up a pattern using self-striping yarn is by changing the colorway. There is a great variety of self-striping yarn available to suit any palette you like.

Another way to change up a project is to throw in a different stitch pattern rather than plain stockinette. Keep in mind, though, that this can change your gauge, so think twice—and swatch!—before you change the stitch pattern on a project that needs to fit a body.

Super-Bulky Rainbow Scarf

The fun thing about using self-striping yarn is that it does all the work for you. The awesome yarn I used for this pattern, Berroco Brio, does even more than make pretty stripes; it also shines with a bit of lustrous fiber. The random thick and thin nature of this yarn adds to its appeal.

Though you can always substitute yarns with similar weights and properties, you should really check this one out if you can. You'll have a showstopper piece that will keep you plenty warm and that you can knit up in no time.

Finished Measurements

5"/13 cm wide x 72"/183 cm long, excluding fringe

Yarn

Berroco Brio, super bulky weight #6 yarn (49% wool, 48% acrylic, 3% other; 109 yd./100 m per 3.5 oz./100 g ball)
- 2 balls #9447 Riot

Needles and Other Materials

- US 15 (10 mm) knitting needles

Adjust needle size as necessary to obtain gauge.

Gauge

11 sts x 12 rows in Moss St = 4"/10 cm square
Gauge is not critical for this project.

Stitch Pattern

Moss Stitch

Rows 1–2: *K1, p1. Repeat from * across.
Rows 3– 4: *P1, k1. Repeat from * across.

Detail of Moss Stitch.

Use a crochet hook to pull the fringe through the edge of your knitting. If necessary/desired, trim fringe so each section is the same length.

Scarf

CO 14 sts.
Work in Moss St for 72"/183 cm.
BO in pattern. Weave in ends.

Fringe

To make fringe, cut pieces of yarn that are 24"/61 cm long. I used 3 pieces for each section of fringe and 8 sections on each side for a total of 48 strands.

Fold each bundle in half, then use a crochet hook to poke through the gap between 2 sts in the last row of knitting. Pull through a loop and pull the ends of the fringe through the loop. Pull tight. Repeat evenly across.

Change It Up

This is a super simple project to modify to make completely unique. One easy way would be to change the stitch pattern. Because this particular yarn is so colorful, it would look great in garter stitch (knit every stitch of every row) or stockinette stitch (knit one row, purl one row), though stockinette has a tendency to curl.

You could also try a simple ribbing pattern like k1, p1 or k2, p2, bearing in mind that you need a multiple of two stitches for single rib and four stitches for double rib.

Or try seed stitch, the even more textured cousin of moss stitch. With a multiple of two stitches, work k1, p1 across for the first two rows, then p1, k1 across for two rows. Repeat these four rows for the pattern.

Eyelet Beret

There are some great self-striping yarns that are made just for knitting socks, but that doesn't mean you can only use them on projects for your feet. The yarn used here has long been in my stash—and I've used it for socks before—but I wanted to illustrate how you can use a great single skein of sock yarn for a different project.

This one is fun, too, because it's worked from the center of the top out, so you can see the progress—and the color play—quickly. Despite the small yarn and needles, this is a fast project and great for gift knitting.

Both the colors and the eyelet design of this hat remind me of flowers, so I'd say this is a great one for your brightest sock yarn and perfect for wearing on rainy spring or fall days.

Finished Measurements

9"/23 cm across the top
14"/35.5 cm around brim, unstretched
To fit a woman.

Yarn

Red Heart Heart & Sole, super fine weight #1 yarn (70%
superwash wool, 30% nylon; 213 yd./195 m per 1.7 oz./50
g ball)
• 1 ball #3960 Spring Stripe

Needles and Other Materials

• US 3 (3.25 mm) set of 4 double-pointed knitting needles
• 6 stitch markers
Adjust needle size as necessary to obtain gauge.

Gauge

24 sts x 32 rnds in St st in the round = 4"/10 cm square

*When you block the hat,
use a plate or piece of
cardboard inside to
hold the round shape
of the hat while
it dries.*

Hat

CO 6 sts.

Kfb each st—12 sts.

Arrange on 3 needles and join in round, being careful not to twist sts.

Rnd 1: Knit.

Rnd 2: *K1, kfb. Repeat from * around—18 sts.

Rnd 3: Knit, placing marker after every 3 sts.

Rnd 4: *M1, k to marker, yo, sm. Repeat from * around—30 sts.

Rnd 5: Knit.

Repeat Rnds 4–5 until each section between markers is 33 sts. If desired, change to a circular needle as needed—198 sts.

Next rnd: *YO, k2tog. Repeat from * around.

Knit 7 rnds.

Next rnd: *YO, k2tog. Repeat from * around.

Knit 7 rnds.

Next rnd: *YO, k2tog. Repeat from * around.

Knit 3 rnds.

Next rnd: *K2tog. Repeat from * to last 2 sts, k2—100 sts.

Work in k1, p1 ribbing for 2"/5 cm.

BO loosely.

Finishing

Use the tail end and a yarn needle to close up the top of the hat, and weave in remaining ends.

It's a great idea to block this hat so that the top will be round. Just give it a soak in some cool water for about fifteen minutes, gently squeeze out all the water you can, then roll it up in a towel to remove excess water. Use a plate or a piece of cardboard cut to size to hold the hat in shape as it dries.

Mock Cable Gloves

I love a simple glove pattern for showing off the beauty of self-striping yarn. This pair is intentionally not a perfect match. I want my projects to be unique and distinctive from store-bought knits. The pretty colors and "unmatched" look give these gloves a funky edge.

The mock cable rib is a somewhat fiddly extra touch that takes these gloves beyond the basic, but you can use regular ribbing if you'd rather.

Finished Measurements

8"/20 cm around

9"/23 cm long from longest fingertip to end of cuff

To fit an average-sized woman.

Yarn

Knit Picks Chroma, fine/fingering weight #2 yarn (70% wool, 30% nylon; 396 yd./362 m per 3.5 oz./100 g ball)
- 1 ball Galapagos

Needles and Other Materials

- US 1 (2.25 mm) set of 4 double-pointed knitting needles
- 2 stitch markers
- Stitch holders or waste yarn

Adjust needle size as necessary to obtain gauge.

Gauge

30 sts x 44 rnds St st in the round = 4"/10 cm square

Pattern Stitch

Mock Cable Rib

Rnds 1–3: *K2, p2. Repeat from * around.

Round 4: *Skip 1 st, k second, leaving on the needle, k skipped st and slip both off needle together, p2. Repeat from * around.

Detail of the Mock Cable Rib pattern on the cuff.

Wrist and Thumb Gusset

CO 60 sts. Divide onto 3 needles and join in round, being careful not to twist sts.

Work in Mock Cable Rib for 7 repeats.

Next rnd: K to last st, M1—61 sts.

Inc rnd: K30, pm, M1, k1, M1, pm, k to end—63 sts.

Next rnd: Knit.

Next rnd: Repeat Inc rnd.

Work Inc rnd every 3 rnds 7 more times—19 gusset sts between markers.

Next rnd: Work to gusset sts, place gusset sts on stitch holder or waste yarn, M1, k to end.

Work even until section above ribbing measures 3.5"/9 cm.

Little Finger

K8, place 46 sts on waste yarn or stitch holder, CO 1, k to end—16 sts for little finger.

Knit until finger measures 2"/5 cm.

*K2tog. Repeat from * around.

Cut yarn and thread on yarn needle. Slip sts onto yarn needle, pulling end through all stitches, closing top of finger tightly.

Ring Finger

Place 46 held sts back on needles. Pick up and knit 2 sts at gap by little finger—48 sts.

Knit for .25"/.6 cm.

K8, place all but last 8 sts on holder, CO 2 over gap—18 sts.

Knit for 2.5"/6 cm.

*K2tog. Repeat from * around.

Cut yarn and thread on yarn needle. Slip sts onto yarn needle, pulling end through all stitches, closing top of finger tightly.

Middle Finger

Place 8 sts from each end of the held sts onto working needles. Pick up and knit 2 sts along edge of ring finger and CO 2 over gap—20 sts.

Knit for 2.75"/7 cm.

*K2tog. Repeat from * around.   (continued)

Cut yarn and thread on yarn needle. Slip sts onto yarn needle, pulling end through all stitches, closing top of finger tightly.

Index Finger

Place remaining sts on needles. Pick up and knit 2 sts along edge of middle finger—18 sts.
Knit for 2.5"/7 cm.
*K2tog. Repeat from * around.
Cut yarn and thread on yarn needle. Slip sts onto yarn needle, pulling end through all stitches, closing top of finger tightly.

Thumb

Place held gusset sts on needles. Pick up and knit 3 sts along hand edge—22 sts.
Knit for 2"/5 cm.
*K2tog. Repeat from * around.
Cut yarn and thread on yarn needle. Slip sts onto yarn needle, pulling end through all stitches, closing top of finger tightly.
Weave in ends.
Make the second glove in the same manner.

Self-Striping Knee Highs

When the yarn is doing all the work, you might as well let it do a lot of work. With these simple socks, all you have to worry about is decreasing down the leg, which is done in a way that adds the look of a seam along the back of the leg. There's also an optional round of eyelets to include if you want to weave a ribbon through and tie the socks to your legs for extra security and cuteness.

The pattern as presented is for a rather small leg, but don't worry; it's easy to customize your socks and I'll walk you through the whole process. See Making Socks to Fit You on page 17.

Just for fun I used what's called an Eye of Partridge heel flap, which is a little different from the standard flap but is both pretty and durable. Feel free to use a standard two-row repeat heel flap pattern if you prefer. (You'll find it in the patterns for the Boxy Stripe Socks on page 51 and the Polka Dot Socks on page 90.)

Finished Measurements

11"/28 cm around at top of calf and 7"/18 cm at ankle.
Leg is 15"/38 cm to bottom of heel.
Foot is 8.5"/21.5 cm long from back of heel to toes.
*To fit a small woman. See Making Socks to Fit You on page 17
for how to customize the fit to any size.*

Yarn

Knit Picks Felici, super fine weight #1 yarn (75% superwash
merino wool, 25% nylon; 218 yd./200 m per 1.7 oz./50 g
skein)
• 3 skeins Maple Leaves

*A note on yarn usage:
I call for three skeins of yarn
here, though when I weigh
my socks they come out at
97 grams, just below the
weight of two 50-gram
skeins. But I needed three
balls because I knit a gauge
swatch (and you should,
too) and in order to get the
stripes to line up properly. If
your leg needs to be bigger
or longer than mine, you'll
need the extra yarn, too.
Better to be safe than sorry.*

Needles and Other Materials

• US 1 (2.25 mm) set of 4 double-pointed knitting needles
• Stitch marker
• 2 lengths of ribbon for weaving in eyelets (optional)
Adjust needle size as necessary to obtain gauge.

Gauge

31 sts x 42 rnds St st in the round = 4"/10 cm square

Leg

CO 88 sts. Arrange on 3 double-pointed needles and join in
the round, being careful not to twist sts.
Work in k2, p2 ribbing for 2"/5 cm.
Knit 3 rnds.
*K2tog, yo. Repeat from * around (this round is optional).
Knit 1 rnd.
K42, k2tog, pm, ssk, k to end.
Continue in St st, decreasing on each side of marker every
fifth round, until 56 sts remain.
Work even until leg measures 12"/30.5 cm.

Making Socks to Fit You

So much more than shoe size goes into making a great-fitting sock! One of the best things about hand-knit socks is that they can and should be customized for the recipient. That's why the patterns in this book give a basic pattern, but allow you to adjust as needed to make the socks fit you or the intended receipient. Because legs and feet come in lots of sizes, it is much better to individually customize leg and foot sizes than to assume that someone with a small or large foot will have a correspondingly small or large calf. Read on as I walk you through the really simple process of adjusting a sock pattern to make a sock that will be a perfect fit!

With a little bit of math, you can make these (or any other socks) just the right size.

First, take some measurements. You'll need to know your calf (for knee highs) and ankle circumferences, and the desired length of the sock leg and foot, as well as your stitch gauge.

I like a sock that's about 1"/2.5 cm smaller than the actual body measurement because it will cling to the body without being uncomfortable. If you've knit socks before, measure a favorite pair and adjust your measurements accordingly to determine how you want the sock to fit.

CAST ON

Once you know the measurements you want for your sock, multiply those numbers by your gauge. For instance if you wanted a sock that was 12"/30.5 cm in the calf, and your gauge is 7.75 stitches per inch, you'd get 93 stitches (12 x 7.75). To make 2x2 ribbing, you need a multiple of 4 stitches, so you'd want to cast on either 92 or 96 stitches.

RIBBED CUFF

If the sock has a ribbed cuff, work that even.

DECREASES

To determine how much and how often you need to decrease you need to do a bit more math. First, determine how long you want the leg to be (minus any ribbing and leaving a couple of inches straight at the bottom of the leg), the circumference of your leg at the top of the sock, and the circumference of your ankle. Then use your gauge to determine how many stitches you need to decrease to get from one to the other, then divide by the total distance, and plan your decreases similarly to the pattern.

For example, for the Self-Striping Knee Socks, the decreases are taken down the center back of the sock, creating a mock seam. To begin the decreases, find the center point of your stitches. Using 92 sts as an example, half is 46 sts, so your decrease round would be: k44, k2tog, pm, ssk, k the rem sts. I figured that I needed to decrease about 4"/10 cm from 11"/28 cm to 7"/18 cm around. I wanted to make my decreases over about 8"/20 cm in length, because the bottom part of the leg is about the same size as the ankle. Knowing I was getting about 10 rounds per 1"/2.5 cm and decreasing 2 stitches each decrease round, I decided to decrease every 5 rounds, which gave me a decrease rate of 4 stitches per 1"/2.5 cm, exactly what I needed to decrease 32 stitches over 8"/20 cm. Your math might not work out that cleanly, or you may decide to decrease more or less severely.

HEEL

The heel flap is worked on half of the stitches, and I worked mine in the middle of the sock. If you want to do the same, divide your number of stitches at the heel into 4. Knit a quarter of the stitches, then start the heel on half the stitches in the middle. The stitch pattern works the same.

For the heel turn, slip the first stitch of every row. Knit across half the stitches plus 1, ssk, k1, turn.

Sl 1, p5, p2tog, p1, turn.

Each row you work one more stitch than the previous row before the decrease until you've worked all the way across.

GUSSET

Pick up stitches as described in the pattern, picking up appropriate numbers of stitches to accommodate your adjustments, and work the gusset in the same way until you're back to the number of stitches you had before the heel turn.

TOE

Knit to 1.5"/4 cm from desired length (or about to the bottom of the little toe, if you're making them for yourself or someone who can try them on as you knit). Work decreases as given in the pattern until you have half the number of stitches you started with, then decrease every round until you have 10 to 12 sts left. Graft the toe closed.

Heel Flap

K14, then work the heel on the next 28 sts back and forth in rows as follows:

Row 1: Sl 1, *k1, sl 1. Repeat from * to last st, k1.
Row 2: Sl 1, p across.
Row 3: Sl 1, k1, *k1, sl 1. Repeat from * across.
Row 4: Repeat Row 2.

Continue in pattern until heel is roughly square, ending on a WS row.

Turn the Heel

Row 1: Sl 1, k15, ssk, k1, turn.
Row 2: Sl 1, p5, p2tog, p1, turn.
Row 3: Sl 1, k6, ssk, k1, turn.
Row 4: Sl 1, p7, p2tog, p1, turn.
Row 5: Sl 1, k8, ssk, k1, turn.
Row 6: Sl 1, p9, p2tog, p1, turn.
Row 7: Sl 1, k10, ssk, k1, turn.
Row 8: Sl 1, p11, p2tog, p1, turn.
Row 9: Sl 1, k12, ssk, k1, turn.
Row 10: Sl 1, p13, p2tog, p1, turn.
Row 11: Sl 1, k14, ssk, turn.
Row 12: Sl 1, p14, p2tog, turn—16 sts rem.

Gusset

Knit across these 16 sts, then pick up and knit 14 sts across side of heel flap.

Knit across 28 leg sts, then, with an empty needle, pick up and knit 14 sts on the other side of the heel flap (or the same number you picked up on the first side). Knit 8 of the heel stitches onto this needle. This is now the end of the round; place marker. You should have 22 stitches each on needles 1 and 3 and the 28 leg stitches on needle 2.

Rnd 1: Knit.
Rnd 2: Knit to 3 sts from the end of needle 1, ssk, k1. Knit across needle 2 (leg stitches). Needle 3: K1, k2tog, k to end.

Repeat these Rnds 1–2 until 56 sts remain.

Foot and Toe

Knit even in St st until foot is 7"/18 cm from back of heel.

Rnd 1: Knit to 3 sts from the end of needle 1, ssk, k1. On needle 2, k1, ssk, k to 3 sts from end of needle, k2tog, k1. On needle 3, k1, k2tog, k to end.
Rnd 2: Knit.

Repeat Rnds 1–2 until 28 sts rem, then repeat Rnd 1 every round until 12 sts rem.

Place 6 sts each on 2 double-pointed needles and graft the toe closed (see page 98 for step-by-step instructions).

Color Belt Sweater

This is one of the projects in the book that I've wanted to knit for a very long time. I thought it would be fun to start a sweater in the middle, with a sort of belt. The belt is worked flat, then seamed up the back. Stitches are picked up for each portion of the top and worked separately, then the "skirt" is picked up and knit in the round, increasing into an A-line shape. Finally, the side and shoulder seams are sewn and stitches are picked up and worked down for the sleeves.

It's a project that never stops moving, and the yarn is a perfect match. I really love the way this one turned out and I hope you'll love it, too.

Finished Measurements

32 (34, 36, 38, 40)"/81.25 (86.5, 91.5, 96.5, 101.5) cm around
the chest

56 (59, 62, 65, 68.5)"/142.25 (150, 157.5, 165, 174) cm around
the bottom

22.75 (23, 23.75, 24, 24.75)"/57.75 (58.5, 60.5, 61, 63) cm long

Yarn

Noro Silk Garden, medium weight #4 yarn (45% silk, 45%
mohair, 10% wool; 110 yd./100 m per 1.7 oz./50 g skein)
- 10 (10, 11, 12, 13) skeins #87 Rainbow

Needles and Other Materials

- US 7 (4.5 mm) 30"/80 cm long circular knitting needle
- US 7 (4.5 mm) straight knitting needles (optional)
- US 7 (4.5 mm) set of 4 double-pointed knitting needles
- 5 stitch markers, 2 each of the same color and 1 other

Adjust needle size as necessary to obtain gauge.

Gauge

18 sts x 26 rnds in St st in the round = 4"/10 cm square

Pattern Stitch

Linen Stitch
Row 1: *K1, sl 1 with yarn in front. Repeat from * to last st, k1.
Row 2: *P1, sl 1 with yarn in back. Repeat from * to last st, p1.

Belt

Using straight needles or two DPNs as desired, CO 12 (12,
14, 14, 16) sts.

Work in Linen St for 32 (34, 36, 38, 40)"/81.25 (86.5, 91.5,
96.5, 101.5) cm.

BO. Sew cast on and bound off edges together, making
a loop.

Finished Measurements

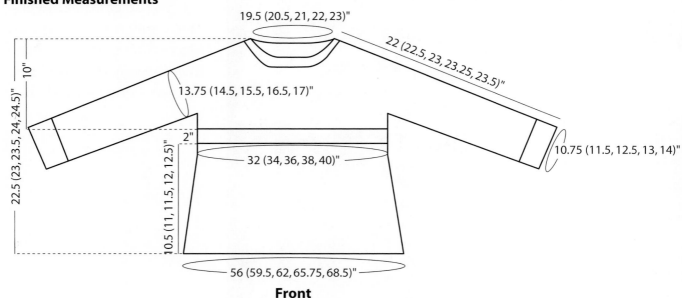

Front

Sew the Linen Stitch belt together to form a loop. The seam will become the center back of the sweater.

Pick up and knit stitches along the belt to begin knitting the rest of the sweater.

Front Top

Fold the belt so that the seam becomes the center back of the sweater. Working on what will be the front top, pick up and knit 72 (76, 80, 84, 88) sts across the front half of the belt.

Work in St st for 3 (3.25, 3.5, 3.75, 4)"/7.75 (8.25, 9, 9.5, 10) cm, ending on a WS row.

ARMHOLE SHAPING

Row 1: BO 4 (4, 5, 5, 6) sts, knit to end of row.
Row 2: BO 4 (4, 5, 5, 6) sts, purl to end of row.
Row 3: Ssk, k to last st, k2tog.
Row 4: Purl.
Work Rows 3–4 a total of 4 (5, 5, 6, 6) times—56 (58, 60, 62, 64) sts.
Work even until piece measures 5 (5.5, 5.75, 6, 6.25)"/12.75 (14, 14.5, 15.25, 16) cm, ending on a WS row.

NECK SHAPING

K22 (23, 24, 25, 26), BO 12 sts, knit across.
Working on just this side of the neck, dec 1 st each RS row (k1, ssk, k across) until 12 sts rem.
Work even until 10"/25.5 cm from where stitches were picked up. BO.
Reattach yarn to the other side and dec 1 st each RS row (work to last 3 sts, k2tog, k1) until 12 sts rem.
Work even until 10"/25.5 cm from where stitches were picked up. BO.

Back Top

Work as for front through Armhole Shaping.
Work even until piece measures 8 (8.5, 8.75, 9, 9.25)"/20.5
(21.75, 22.25, 23, 23.5) cm, ending on a WS row.

NECK SHAPING

K16 (17, 18, 19, 20), BO 24 sts, k across.
Working on just this side of the neck, dec 1 st each RS row
(k1, ssk, k across) until 12 sts rem.
Work even until 10"/25.5 cm from where stitches were
picked up. BO.
Repeat on the other side, reattaching the yarn and dec
1 st each RS row (work to last 3 sts, k2tog, k1) until
12 sts remain.

Bottom

Using circular needle, pick up and knit 144 (152, 160, 168,
176) sts around the entire belt. Join in the round, being
careful not to twist the sts.
Knit in the round for 1"/2.5 cm.
Next rnd: *K4, M1. Repeat from * around—180 (190, 200,
210, 220) sts.
Knit for 2"/5 cm.
Next rnd: *K5, M1. Repeat from * around—216 (228, 240,
252, 264) sts.
Knit for 3"/7.75 cm.
Next rnd: *K6, M1. Repeat from * around—252 (266, 280,
294, 308) sts.
Sizes 34 and 38 only: K6, M1, knit rem sts and M1 at end of
rnd—2 sts increased, 268 sts for size 34 and 296 sts for
size 38.
Knit for 4"/10 cm.
Work in k2, p2 ribbing for 2"/5 cm. BO in pattern.
Sew the underarm and shoulder seams before knitting
the sleeves.

Sleeves

Using DPNs and starting at the bottom of the underarm,
pick up and knit 62 (66, 70, 74, 78) sts for sleeve. Place
markers after 11 (12, 13, 14, 15) sts (first color), 11 (12, 13,
14, 15) sts (second color), 18 (18, 18, 18, 18) sts (second
color), 11 (12, 13, 14, 15) sts (first color), 11 (12, 13, 14, 15)
sts (end of round, can be any color).
Knit to the second marker in the second color, sm, wrap
and turn.
Knit back to other second color marker, sm, wrap and turn.
Knit to the wrapped stitch, knit it along with its wrap, knit 1
st, wrap and turn.
Repeat this row until you reach the first color markers. End
on a WS row.
Begin to work in the round, removing markers (other than
the end of round marker) as you come to them and
working wrapped stitches together with their wraps.

Knit 6 rnds even.
Dec rnd: K1, k2tog, k to 3 sts from end, ssk, k1.
Repeat Dec rnd every seventh round a total of 7 times—48
(52, 56, 60, 64) sts.
Work even until sleeve measures 20 (20.5, 21, 21.25,
21.5)"/51 (52, 53.5, 54, 54.75) cm from top of shoulder.
Work in k2, p2 ribbing for 2"/5 cm.
BO in pattern.
Work second sleeve in the same manner.

Neckline

Using DPNs and starting at right shoulder, pick up and knit
88 (92, 96, 100, 104) sts evenly around neckline (making
sure you get a multiple of 4).
Work in k2, p2 ribbing for 1"/2.5 cm.
BO loosely in pattern.
Weave in ends. Block.

Making Your Own Stripes

Stripes are an easy way to add color to a knitting project without a lot of effort. All you have to do to change colors at the end of a row or round is drop the first color and start knitting with the second.

If your stripes are just a few rows or rounds wide—especially if you're knitting something where the back is hidden—it's perfectly acceptable to leave the first yarn attached to the work and carry it up as you go along to the place where you will need it again. To carry the yarn up the work, when you change colors, just pick the new working yarn up from underneath the old one. Every few rows or rounds thereafter, twist the colors together at the end of the row or round to continue to carry the non-working yarn up the knitted item. Continue changing colors and carrying the non-working yarn in this manner.

If you're working really long stripes or just don't want those carries to show, feel free to cut the yarn, leaving a long tail, each time you change colors. Weave in the ends as you go or at the end.

Stripes can be worked in just about any width you want, though the standard is to work at least two rows in each color when working flat so that color changes will always occur at the same side of your knitting, where your working yarn will be waiting (allowing for carrying yarn and avoiding ends to weave in). When working in the round, stripes can be any width you like. It's actually a lot of fun to knit one-round stripes, and it gives a different look to your knitting.

When working stockinette stitch, you'll end up with crisp stripes if you always change colors on the right side (the smooth, knit side). You can also purposefully change colors on the wrong side of the work or in a textured stitch pattern. The purl bumps will break up the color, which can produce interesting effects.

Pros of Knitting Your Own Stripes

- You have all the control over which colors you use and how much of them you use.
- It's a great way to play with and learn about color.
- If you're knitting a small project with stripes, it can be a great way to use up little leftover bits of yarn.

Experiment with your stripes! Here, I tried adding purl rounds to make the stripes pop.

Wh
en knitting stripes in the round, as in all of the patterns presented here except for the scarf, you will be presented with the problem that's known as jogs. Because circular knitting is actually a spiral, the beginnings and ends of rows don't line up, which doesn't matter when you're knitting with one color but can be downright glaring when knitting stripes.

There are several possible ways to deal with the jog, shown in the photo from the bottom up.

My favorite is to knit the first round of the new color as usual, then slip the first stitch of the second round as if to purl. This pulls the new color up a bit, but it's still somewhat noticeable because of that elongated slipped stitch.

Another popular method is to knit the first round of a new color as normal, but at the beginning of the second round, lift up the stitch below the first stitch (which will be in the first color) and then knit those two stitches together. This makes an elongated stitch, too, so it's just a matter of preference which method you use.

You can also knit the project as usual, without addressing the jogs until the knitting is complete. Then, while weaving in the yarn ends, use duplicate stitch to cover that stitch that looks like it was knit the wrong color with the right color.

Ways to Knit Jogless Stripes

There are a few ways to hide jogs in your striped knitting. Shown from the bottom up: 1. Slip-stitch fix. 2. Lift-stitch fix. 3. Duplicate stitch.

Cons of Knitting Your Own Stripes

- When knitting in the round, which actually produces a spiral, the stripes won't line up perfectly at the beginning and end of the round. There are ways to make this problem less obvious (see above), but it's still a big potential con.
- More ends to weave in than self-striping yarn projects.
- When finishing a project knit flat, you have to take extra care to make sure the stripes line up across different parts of the project.

How to Make a Striped Project Your Own

Stripe-it-yourself projects are easy to personalize through color, because you can easily choose any two, three, or more colors you like without a lot of worry.

Another easy way to change a project is to make the stripes narrower, wider, random, or use more or fewer colors than the project calls for. When I was designing the sweater for this chapter, I did a lot of swatching to determine how wide I wanted the stripes to be and in what order I liked the colors most. I even experimented with knitting a purl round on the right side to break up the stripes. (You can see some of my swatches on page 23.)

If you want to alter a striped pattern, even if you're just changing colors, you'll want to swatch to make sure you like the look before you proceed with the full project.

Sunburst Horizontal Stripe Scarf

t's fun and easy to make your own stripes, and it's interesting to see what happens when you throw a different stitch pattern or construction method into the mix. This project is worked sideways, or the long way, and you use each color for just one row, leaving long tails at each end that become the fringe. It's a really easy but different way to work a scarf, and single-stripe rows in garter stitch look a lot more interesting than garter stitch stripes worked vertically would.

I used three colors for my version, but you could easily make this a stash-busting project and work each row in a different color. I've done that, too, with shades of the same color, and it was really beautiful.

I also made this a bit of a skinny scarf, which means you can knit a couple of scarves from one skein of each color. Or make it wider if you like.

Shown with Color-Block Striped Sweater

Finished Measurements

3"/7.5 cm wide x 64"/162.5 cm long, including fringe

Yarn

Halcyon Yarn Botanica, medium weight #4 yarn (100% wool; 160 yd./146 m per 4 oz./113 g hank)
- 1 hank #9 Red (Color A)
- 1 hank #7 Orange (Color B)
- 1 hank #43 Gold (Color C)

Needles and Other Materials

- US 8 (5 mm) circular knitting needle, at least 36"/90 cm long, but longer is better

Adjust needle size as necessary to obtain gauge.

Gauge

16 sts x 32 rows in garter st = 4"/10 cm square
Gauge is not critical for this project.

Scarf

With Color A, and leaving a tail of about 12"/31.5 cm, CO 150 sts. Leave a 12"/31.5 cm tail on the other side and cut the yarn.

Row 1: Leaving a 12"/31.5 cm tail, knit 1 row in B. Leave a 12"/31.5 cm tail on the other side and cut the yarn.

Row 2: Leaving a 12"/31.5 cm tail, knit 1 row in C. Leave a 12"/31.5 cm tail on the other side and cut the yarn.

Row 3: Leaving a 12"/31.5 cm tail, knit 1 row in A. Leave a 12"/31.5 cm tail on the other side and cut the yarn.

Repeat Rows 1–3 until piece is about 3"/7.5 cm wide, ending with color C.

BO in A, leaving a 12"/31.5 cm tail on each side.

Fringe

You can tie the tails together if you like, or just let them hang. I tied six pieces together in each section (the last section has seven).

Ombre Striped Mitts

sing different shades of the same color is sure to create a harmonious effect. Here I used four shades of blue, working from the cuff up and from lightest to darkest. A little cable panel down the back of the arm makes these a little more fun to knit and to wear, and the length makes them a great addition to an outfit with short sleeves. When the air conditioning goes on, so do these mitts!

Shown with Two-Color Cable Hat

Finished Measurements

9.5"/24 cm around at cuff
7"/18 cm around at hand
12"/30 cm long, excluding fingers
To fit an average-sized woman.

Yarn

Lion Brand Martha Stewart Crafts Extrasoft Wool Blend, medium weight #4 yarn (65% acrylic, 35% wool; 165 yd./150 m per 3.5 oz./100 g skein)

- 1 skein Igloo (Color A)
- 1 skein Winter Sky (Color B)
- 1 skein Blue Corn (Color C)
- 1 skein Sailor Blue (Color D)

Needles and Other Materials

- US 7 (4.5 mm) set of 4 double-pointed knitting needles
- Cable needle or extra DPN
- Stitch holder

Adjust needle size as necessary to obtain gauge.

Gauge

17 sts x 26 rnds in St st in the round = 4"/10 cm square
Gull Stitch panel = 2"/5 cm wide

Pattern Stitch

Gull Stitch

Rnd 1: P2, k6, p2.
Rnd 2: K4, sl 2, k4.
Rnd 3: P2, k2, sl 2, p2, k2.
Rnd 4: K2, sl 2 to cable needle or DPN and hold in back, k1, k2 from cable needle, sl 1 onto cable needle and hold in front, k2, k1 from cable needle, k2.
Repeat Rnds 1–4 for pattern.

Right Mitt

With Color A, CO 48 stitches, divide evenly on 3 DPNs, and join to work in the round.
Work in k2, p2 ribbing for 1"/2.5 cm.
Pattern rnd: K19, work Gull St panel, k19.
Repeat Pattern Rnd for 1 full repeat of the Gull St pattern.
Next rnd: Knit to 3 sts before the panel, ssk, k1, work the next round of Gull St in sequence, k1, k2tog, k to end of round—2 sts dec.
Continue to work the pattern as established, decreasing 2 sts every 6 rnds until 32 sts remain. *At the same time,* change colors from lightest to darkest every 3"/8 cm, ending each color section with Rnd 4.
On the first rnd of the fourth color section (Color D), work across the panel, k2, sl 6 sts onto holder, CO 6 sts and work across.

Work pattern as established for 3"/8 cm more, then cut yarn.

FINGERS

Starting with Color A and the stitches closest to the thumb, move 9 sts (4 from one side of the mitt, 5 from the other) to 2 DPNs and k2, p2, k2tog, k1, p2. Work in k2, p2 ribbing for 3 rnds. BO in pattern.
Repeat with Color B for middle finger.
Using Color C for ring finger, work on 8 sts. Work k2, p2 ribbing for 3 rnds. BO in pattern.
Using Color D for little finger, work on 5 sts. K2, p2tog, p1. Then work k2, p2 ribbing for 2 rnds. BO in pattern.
Using Color D for thumb, knit across held stitches, then pick up and knit 6 sts (12 sts total). Work k2, p2 ribbing for 4 rnds. BO in pattern.
Weave in ends.

Left Mitt

Work as for right, except as follows: On the first round of the fourth color section, k2, sl 6 sts onto holder, CO 6 sts and work across.
Work the rest of the mitt as for the right mitt.

Shown with Two-Color Cable Hat

Welted Stripe Hat

I like to play with textures in stripes to give them a different look. In this case the red stripes are worked in stockinette stitch and the green are in reverse stockinette, making for a fun fabric that folds in on itself. This hat may feel like it takes longer to knit than it should because you gain length a little more slowly as it folds up in the welts. But it's a really cute look that will stretch to fit a variety of heads.

Finished Measurements

20"/51 cm around
7"/18 cm long, unstretched; 9"/23 cm long, stretched

Yarn

Berroco Ultra Alpaca, medium/worsted weight #4 yarn
   (50% alpaca, 50% wool; 215 yd./196 m per 3.5 oz./100 g
   skein)
- 1 skein #52181 Ruby Mix (Color A)
- 1 skein #6262 Snap Pea (Color B)

Needles and Other Materials

- US 7 (4.5 mm) set of 5 double-pointed needles
- US 7 (4.5 mm) 16"/40 cm long circular needle (optional; I
   worked the whole hat on DPNs, but you can start with a
   circular needle and switch to DPNs when the circumference gets too small, if you'd rather)
Adjust needle sizes as necessary to obtain gauge.

Gauge

16 sts x 40 rnds in Welt Pattern = 4"/10 cm square

Pattern Stitch

Welt Pattern
Rnds 1–3: Purl in Color B.
Rnds 4–8: Knit in Color A.
Repeat for pattern.

Hat

Using Color A, CO 80 sts. Divide onto 4 needles and join in round, being careful not to twist sts.

Work in k1, p1 ribbing for 1"/2.5 cm.

Knit 1 rnd.

Switch to Color B and begin Welt Pattern.

Work full pattern 5 times, then repeat Color B rnds.

Switch to Color A and *k6, k2tog. Repeat from * around.

Next rnd: Knit.

Next rnd: *K5, k2tog. Repeat from * around.

Next rnd: Knit.

Next rnd: *K4, k2tog. Repeat from * around.

Next rnd: Knit.

Next rnd: *K3, k2tog. Repeat from * around.

Next rnd: Knit.

Next rnd: *K2, k2tog. Repeat from * around.

Next rnd: Knit.

Next rnd: *K1, k2tog. Repeat from * around.

Next rnd: *K2tog. Repeat from * around—10 sts.

Cut yarn, leaving a long tail. Thread yarn onto yarn needle, slip sts onto yarn and pull tight.

Weave in ends.

Swim Lesson Socks

These simple ribbed socks have a funny name because they have a story. While I was working on this book, my daughter, who was four at the time, was taking swim lessons for a couple of weeks. I needed a really easy pattern I could knit poolside, and because it was summer these short socks were the result.

The ribbed leg means they'll fit a range of sizes, and I like the combination of a solid color and a mottled one to add a little more interest. Just for fun I did a short row heel on these, but feel free to work a more standard heel flap and gusset (see Self-Striping Knee Highs on page 15 or Boxy Stripe Socks on page 51 for instructions) if you'd rather.

Shown with
Diamond Circular
Yoke Sweater

Finished Measurements

7.5"/19 cm around leg and foot
Foot is 9"/23 cm long from toe to back of heel
Leg is 5.5"/14 cm long from cuff to bottom of heel
*To fit an average woman. See Making Socks to Fit You on page
17 for how to customize the fit to any size.*

Yarn

SWTC Tofutsies, fine/sock weight #2 yarn (50% superwash
wool, 25% Soysilk, 22.5% cotton, 2.5% chitin; 465 yd./425
m per 3.5 oz./100 g skein)
• 1 skein #943 Brown (Color A)
• 1 skein #733 Reds (Color B)

Needles and Other Materials

• US 1 (2.25 mm) set of 4 double-pointed knitting needles
Adjust needle size as necessary to obtain gauge.

Gauge

34 sts x 46 rnds in St st in the round = 4"/10 square

Leg

With Color A, CO 64 sts. Divide onto double-pointed nee-
   dles and join in rnd, being careful not to twist sts.
Work in k2, p2 ribbing for 1"/2.5 cm.
Change to Color B and work in k2, p2 ribbing for 1"/2.5 cm.
Change to Color A and work in k2, p2 ribbing for 1"/2.5 cm.

Heel

Change to Color B for heel, which is worked back and forth
   in rows on 32 sts.
Row 1: K31, wrap and turn.
Row 2: P30, wrap and turn.
Row 3: Knit to 1 st before last wrapped st, wrap and turn.
Row 4: Purl to 1 st before last wrapped st, wrap and turn.
Repeat Rows 3–4, working 1 fewer st each row, until 10 sts
   are unworked in the middle.
Next row: Work to first wrapped st, work the st along with
   its wrap, wrap and turn. This st now has 2 wraps.
Continue across, working the first wrapped stitch on each
   row and wrapping sts again as you come to them until all
   sts in heel have been worked. When you get to the end of
   the heel sts, wrap the first st on either end of the leg sts.

Foot

Go back to working in rnds, with half of the sts for the bottom of the foot on needle 1, the other half on needle 2,
   and the top of the foot on needle 3. The side of the foot is
   now the end of the round.
Work in St st in Color B for 1"/2.5 cm.
Change to Color A and knit 1"/2.5 cm.
Continue to alternate colors every inch for 5"/13 cm (or
   until sock is 2"/5 cm from desired length).

Toe

Continue to alternate colors every inch as you work the toe.
Rnd 1: Needle 1: K1, ssk, k to end. Needle 2: K to 3 sts from
   end, k2tog, k1. Needle 3: Ssk, k to 3 sts from end, k2tog, k1.
Rnd 2: Knit 1 rnd.
Repeat Rnds 1–2 until 32 sts rem.
Next rnd: Knit.
Repeat Rnd 1 every rnd until 8 sts rem.
Cut yarn, leaving a long tail. Thread onto yarn needle and
   graft the toe closed (see page 98 for step-by-step instruc-
   tions on grafting).
Knit the second sock in the same manner.

Color-Block Striped Raglan Sweater

knew I wanted to include a raglan sweater in this collection because it's such a classic shape, and it's pretty fun to knit, too. Adding stripes after the raglan shaping is done makes it a little more interesting to knit the body, but make sure you end the round under an arm so the changing of colors isn't so noticeable.

I worked my sleeves in the solid blue color, but you may wish to work them in stripes as well. If that's the case, pick up an extra skein of each stripe color, just in case.

Finished Measurements

Chest is 36 (38, 40, 42, 44)"/91.5 (96.5, 101.5, 106.75, 111.75) cm around

21 (22, 22.5, 23.25, 24)"/53.5 (56, 57, 59, 61) cm long

To fit a 34 (36, 38, 40, 42)"/86.5 (91.5, 96.5, 101.5, 106.5) cm chest

Yarn

Cascade 220, medium/worsted weight #4 yarn (100% Peruvian Highland wool; 220 yd./200 m per 3.5 oz./100 g skein)

- 3 (3, 4, 4, 4) skeins #9420 Como Blue (Color A)
- 1 (1, 1, 1, 2) skein(s) #9466 Zinnia Red (Color B)
- 1 (1, 1, 1, 2) skein(s) #7826 California Poppy (Color C)
- 1 (1, 1, 1, 2) skein(s) #9495, Harvest (Color D)

Needles and Other Materials

- US 7 (4.5 mm) circular knitting needles with 16"/40 cm and 30"/80 cm cables
- US 6 (4 mm) 30"/80 cm long circular knitting needle
- US 7 (4.5 mm) set of 4 double-pointed knitting needles
- US 6 (4 mm) set of 4 double-pointed knitting needles
- 4 locking stitch markers
- 2 stitch holders or waste yarn

Adjust needle sizes as necessary to obtain gauge.

Gauge

19 sts x 26 rnds in St st on larger needles = 4"/10 cm square

Notes

- Sweater is worked top-down in rows to begin, and then in the round.

Finished Measurements

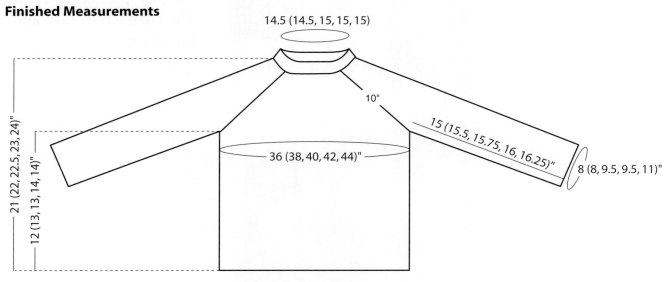

14.5 (14.5, 15, 15, 15)

10"

15 (15.5, 15.75, 16, 16.25)"

8 (8, 9.5, 9.5, 11)"

36 (38, 40, 42, 44)"

21 (22, 22.5, 23, 24)"

12 (13, 13, 14, 14)"

Front

Cast On and Place Markers

With Color A and the shorter size 7 US circular needle, CO 46 (56, 62, 74, 78) sts. Place stitch markers as follows for your size:

Size 34

Sts 2, 11, 36, and 45 (1 front, 1 raglan seam, 8 sleeve, 1 raglan seam, 24 back, 1 raglan seam, 8 sleeve, 1 raglan seam, 1 front).

Size 36

Sts 4, 15, 42, 53 (3 front, 1 raglan seam, 10 sleeve, 1 raglan seam, 26 back, 1 raglan seam, 10 sleeve, 1 raglan seam, 3 front).

Size 38

Sts 4, 17, 46, 59 (3 front, 1 raglan seam, 12 sleeve, 1 raglan seam, 28 back, 1 raglan seam, 12 sleeve, 1 raglan seam, 3 front).

Size 40

Sts 6, 21, 54, 69 (5 front, 1 raglan seam, 14 sleeve, 1 raglan seam, 32 back, 1 raglan seam, 14 sleeve, 1 raglan seam, 5 front).

Size 41

Sts 6, 23, 56, 73 (5 front, 1 raglan seam, 16 sleeve, 1 raglan seam, 32 back, 1 raglan seam, 16 sleeve, 1 raglan seam, 5 front).

Raglan Increases

Row 1 (WS): Purl.

Row 2 (RS): K1 (3, 3, 5, 5), M1, yo, k1, yo, k8 (10, 12, 14, 16), yo, k1, yo, k24 (26, 28, 32, 32), yo, k1, yo, k8 (10, 12, 14, 16), yo, k1, yo, M1, k1 (3, 3, 5, 5)—10 sts inc.

Repeat Rows 1 and 2 continuing to M1 after first st and before last st of each RS row, while also working a yo on each side of the four raglan seams (the marked sts) of each RS row (you can remove the markers as soon as you get the hang of it). Continue in this manner for 14 (16, 16, 16, 16) total rows—116 (136, 142, 154, 158) sts (about 2.25"/5.75 cm).

Purl 1 row.

JOIN WORK

Knit across next RS row and CO 8 (8, 8, 10, 12) sts at end. Join in the round, being careful not to twist the sts—124 (144, 150, 164, 170) sts; 38 (46, 46, 52, 54) front sts, 1 seam st, 22 (26, 28, 30, 32) sleeve sts, 1 seam st, 38 (42, 44, 48, 48) back sts, 1 seam st, 22 (26, 28, 30, 32) sleeve sts, 1 seam st.

COMPLETE RAGLAN INCREASES

Continue to work only the yo raglan seam increases every other round for 21 (20, 22, 22, 24) more raglan increase rnds. Piece will measure about 9 (9, 10, 10, 10)"/23 (23, 25.5, 25.5, 25.5) cm. End with a non-increase round—292 (304, 326, 340, 362) sts; 80 (86, 90, 96, 102) front sts, 1 seam st, 64 (66, 72, 74, 80) sleeve sts, 1 seam st, 80 (82, 88, 92, 96) back sts, 1 seam st, 64 (66, 72, 74, 80) sleeve sts, 1 seam st.

SEPARATE SLEEVES

Next rnd: Knit to the first st beyond the raglan sts. Place the next 64 (66, 72, 74, 80) sts on holder for sleeve, CO 2 sts. Repeat with rem sts. Right underarm is now the end of the round—168 (176, 186, 196, 206) sts on needles.

The raglan increases have been made and the sleeve stitches are on scrap yarn.

Body

Switch to Color B and work in St st, changing colors (Color B, C, D, A) every 5 rnds. Work until you have 14 (15, 15, 16, 16) stripes. Piece measures approximately 19.75 (20.5, 21.5, 22.5, 22.5)"/50 (52, 54.5, 57, 57) cm.

Change to smaller needle and work in k2, p1 ribbing for 10 rnds, continuing to change colors as established. BO in pattern with last stripe color.

Sleeves

With larger DPNs and Color A, pick up the 64 (66, 72, 74, 80) held sts around one arm. Then pick up and knit 4 sts along base of armpit—68 (70, 76, 78, 84) sts. Bottom of armpit is beg of rnd.

SLEEVE DECREASES

Dec rnd: K1, k2tog, k to 3 sts from end of rnd, ssk, k1—2 sts dec.

Work Dec rnd every fourth rnd 3 (4, 4, 5, 5) times—62 (62, 68, 68, 74) sts.

Work Dec rnd every fifth rnd 12 times until 38 (38, 44, 44, 50) sts rem.

Work even until sleeve measures 21 (22, 23, 23, 24)"/53.5 (56, 58.5, 58.5, 61) cm from top raglan edge. Inc 1 st in last rnd.

Change to smaller DPNs and work in k2, p1 ribbing for 2"/5 cm. BO in pattern.

Work other sleeve in the same manner.

Neckline

Using the smaller DPNs and starting at the right neck edge, pick up and knit 69 (69, 72, 72, 72) sts evenly around neckline. *Note: The total sts must be divisible by 3 in order to work the ribbing.*

Work in k2, p1 ribbing for 3 rnds.

BO loosely in pattern.

Weave in ends and block.

Slip-Stitch Knitting

feel like people—myself included—don't use slip-stitch knitting as a colorwork technique nearly as often as they should. It's a really easy way to get the look of two different colors in a row or round without actually working with two strands of yarn at a time. Slipping a stitch elongates the stitch and pulls the color from one row or round to the next. So if stitches are knit on the next row in a different color from the slipped stitches, you see both colors in that row. This allows you to make cool patterns that look a lot more complex than they are, while still only working with one color per row.

Making a Slip-Stitch Pattern

Slip-stitch patterns are worked with two colors at a time, but only using one color to knit each row. The patterns are usually geometric and symmetrical, with stitches slipped on one row to bring that color up then worked in the second color on a later row.

The pattern will tell you what color yarn to use on each row and which stitches to slip and which to knit. Stitches are always slipped as if you were purling them—which keeps them from being twisted on the needle—with the yarn toward the back of the work.

Little strands of the unworked color will appear at the base of the slipped stitches on the back of the work, but they aren't too obtrusive. All of the projects here except the scarf hide them on the unseen inside anyway.

Typically you'll change the working yarn color every couple of rows, which means you can just carry the unused yarn up the side as you go.

Pros of Slip-Stitch Knitting

- This is a really easy way to get more color into your knitting projects, because it's no more intimidating than knitting regular stripes.
- You don't usually have to read or follow a chart. The stitch pattern is explained in the text of the pattern.
- Carrying yarns up the side of the work means fewer ends to weave in.
- Projects look more complicated than they are.

Cons of Slip-Stitch Knitting

- You have to pay a little attention to make sure you're slipping the right stitches and knitting with the right color each row or round.
- Floats of yarn on the back of the work may bother you.
- You need to keep your tension even as you slip stitches so that the strands on the back don't get too tight.
- Floats can make a project a little stiffer and warmer than it would be otherwise.

Stitches are always slipped purlwise with the yarn toward the back of the work.

Making a Slip-Stitch Pattern Your Own

Slip-stitch patterns can easily be modified with the help of a stitch dictionary that includes slip-stitch patterns, or by playing with slip stitches on your own. The pattern on the socks here is one I came up with while playing around, though it's probably published elsewhere, too.

As you get more comfortable with slip-stitch patterns you'll want to play with them and try to develop your own patterns, too.

You can also try experimenting with a special kind of slip-stitch knitting known as mosaic knitting. This technique was brought into popular knitting knowledge (as so many things were) by Barbara G. Walker, who published her book on the subject, called *Mosaic Knitting*, in 1976.

These patterns are particularly unique because they can be worked on any number of stitches in garter or stockinette stitch. Colors are changed after two rows, and the patterns range from simple, small repeats that could easily be substituted into these basic patterns to much bigger designs that are perfect for afghan blocks or, indeed, whole blankets.

The key is to make sure that your chosen stitch pattern will fit evenly into the number of stitches needed for the project and that you're still getting the same gauge as given in the pattern (this is especially true for garments that need to fit the body correctly).

As usual you can also work projects with more or fewer colors, or change the look by switching which color is the background and which makes the pattern—which can make a big difference, as you'll see in the scarf project here.

Slip-stitch patterns, such as the one used in the Boxy Stripe Socks, are a fun and easy way to add interest to stripes.

Brick Stitch Scarf

One of my all-time favorite slip-stitch patterns is Brick Stitch. It's such a simple repeat you'll have it memorized in no time, but it's really dramatic in bright colors like I used here. I couldn't decide which color I liked best as the "brick" and which as the "mortar," so I switched halfway through. This makes for a fun lesson in color dominance, but you can do it all one way if you'd rather.

Finished Measurements

5.25"/13 cm wide x 8'/2.4 m long

Yarn

Spud & Chloë Sweater, medium weight #4 yarn (55% superwash wool, 45% organic cotton; 160 yd./146 m per 3.5
oz./100 g skein)
- 1 skein #7508 Pollen (Color A)
- 1 skein #7504 Lake (Color B)

Needles and Other Materials

- US 7 (4.5 mm) knitting needles
Adjust needle size as necessary to obtain gauge.

Gauge

17 sts x 28 rows in Brick Stitch = 4"/10 cm square

Pattern Stitch

Brick Stitch
Rows 1–2: With A, knit.
Row 3: With B, k1, *sl 1, k3, repeat from * to last 2 sts, sl 1, k1.
Row 4: With B, p1, *sl 1, p3, repeat from * to last 2 sts, sl 1, p1.
Rows 5–6: With A, knit.
Row 7: With B, k3, *sl 1, k3. Repeat from * across.
Row 8: With B, p3, *sl 1, p3. Repeat from * across.
Repeat Rows 1–8 for pattern.

Scarf

With Color A, CO 23 sts.
Work Brick St pattern for 48"/122 cm.
If desired, exchange Color A and Color B; knit another
   48"/122 cm in pattern.
BO.
Weave in ends.

Note: I started with yellow as Color A and Blue as Color B and switched halfway through.

Chain Stripe Hat

A s soon as I started thinking about including slip-stitch knitting in this book, I knew I wanted to do a pattern with chain stripes. This bold pattern is usually worked as shown, with three colors, but you could also make this a stash-busting project by working each "chain" in a different color.

Either way, this is an easy pattern to master and a great illustration of the power of slip stitches.

This combination of colors reminds me of a sunny day in summer, but choose any three (or more) colors you like for a striking hat all your own.

Shown with Sunburst Horizontal Stripe Scarf

Finished Measurements

19"/48 cm around
8"/20 cm tall
To fit snugly on an adult female.

Yarn

Plymouth Yarns Galway Worsted, medium/worsted weight #4 yarn (100% wool; 210 yd./192 m per 3.5 oz./100 g skein)

- 1 skein #17 Kelly Green (Color A)
- 1 skein #91 Clementine Orange (Color B)
- 1 skein #147 Hot Neon Yellow (Color C)

Needles and Other Materials

- US 8 (5 mm) 16"/40 cm long circular needle
- US 8 (5 mm) set of 4 double-pointed knitting needles

Adjust needle size as necessary to obtain gauge.

Gauge

18.5 sts x 32 rnds in Chain Stripe Pattern in the round = 4"/10 cm square

Pattern Stitch

Chain Stripe
Rnds 1–2: With A, knit.
Rnd 3: With B, knit.
Rnd 4: With B, purl.
Rnds 5–6: With A, *k6, sl 2. Repeat from * around.
Rnd 7: With B, repeat Rnd 5.
Rnd 8: With B, purl.
Rnds 9–10: With A, knit.
Rnd 11: With C, knit.
Rnd 12: With C, purl.
Rnds 13–14: With A, k2, *sl 2, k6, repeat from * to last 6 sts, sl 2, k4.
Rnd 15: With C, repeat Rnd 13.
Rnd 16: With C, purl.
Repeat Rnds 1–16 for pattern.

Hat

With Color A, CO 88 sts.

Work in k2, p2 ribbing for 2"/5 cm.

Work 2 full repeats of the Chain Stripe Pattern (hat should measure about 6"/15 cm from the cast on edge).

Work Rnd 1 of Chain Stripe Pattern.

Next rnd: *K9, k2tog. Repeat from * around—80 sts.

Note: Change to double-pointed needles as needed.

Work Rnds 3–9 of Chain Stripe Pattern.

Next rnd: *K3, k2tog. Repeat from * around—64 sts.

Work Rnds 11–16 of Chain Stripe Pattern.

Change to Color A.

Next rnd: *K2, k2tog. Repeat from * around—48 sts.

Next rnd: Knit.

Next rnd: *K1, k2tog. Repeat from * around—32 sts.

Next 2 rnds: *K2tog. Repeat from * around—8 sts.

Leaving a long tail, cut the yarn. Thread onto a yarn needle, slip the remaining sts onto the yarn and pull tight.

Weave in ends.

Lattice Mitts

I love this sweet pattern and these cute little mitts, perfect for a garden party or whenever you need to keep your hands warm. They leave your fingers free but cover your thumb nicely, providing a nice balance between mobility and warmth.

I chose this pattern to illustrate the color principle of working with two shades of the same color. Use a lighter and darker version of whatever color you like to make mitts you'll love to wear.

These mitts are identical so you can wear either one on either hand.

Finished Measurements

6 (7)"/15 (18) cm circumference
8"/20 cm long
To fit a teenager to small woman (average-sized woman).

Yarn

Debbie Bliss Cashmerino Aran, medium weight #4 yarn
   (55% merino wool, 33% microfiber acrylic, 12% cash-
   mere; 99 yd./90 m per 1.7 oz./50 g ball)
- 1 ball #46 Heather (Color A)
- 1 ball #55 Blackberry (Color B)

Needles and Other Materials

- US 8 (5 mm) set of 4 double-pointed knitting needles
- Stitch holder or waste yarn
Adjust needle size as necessary to obtain gauge.

Gauge

20 sts x 26 rnds in Lattice Pattern in the round = 4"/10 cm

Pattern Stitch

Lattice Pattern (in the round)

Rnds 1–2: With B, *k4, sl 2. Repeat from * around.
Rnd 3: With A, *k4, sl 2. Repeat from * around.
Rnd 4: With A, *p4, sl 2. Repeat from * around.
Rnds 5–6: With B, *sl 2, k4. Repeat from * around.
Rnd 7: With A, *sl 2, k4. Repeat from * around.
Rnd 8: With A, *sl2, p4. Repeat from * around.
Repeat Rnds 1–8 for pattern.

Note: This is how the pattern is worked in the round; it won't come out right if you try to knit your swatch flat.

Mitt

With Color A, CO 30 (36) sts. Divide evenly onto DPNs and join to work in the round, being careful not to twist sts.
Work in k1, p1 ribbing for 1"/2.5 cm.
Work in Lattice Pattern until piece measures 5"/13 cm.

THUMB GUSSET

Continuing in pattern, work across 12 (18) stitches, CO 2 sts using backward loop CO for thumb gusset, work across.
Work thumb gusset in St st in whatever color you're using for that round. Inc 1 st (kfb or M1) at each end of the gusset each round until it has 10 (12) sts.
Continue straight until thumb is 20 rounds (10 stripes) long. Place gusset sts on a holder.
Work 4 more rounds on mitt body only.
With Color A, work in k1, p1 ribbing for 2 rnds. BO.
Place thumb stitches back on needles. With Color A, work in k1, p1 ribbing for 2 rnds. BO.
Weave in ends.
Knit second mitt in same manner.

Boxy Stripe Socks

This slip-stitch pattern is something I came up with while playing around with other patterns, but I'm sure I didn't invent it. This is a really good first slip-stitch project because you're only slipping stitches on two rounds of the repeat; the rest is just stripes.

I like the subtlety of this pattern in two colors that are close to each other on the color wheel, but you could do it with complementary colors or even black or brown plus a bright color for a completely different look.

Finished Measurements

8"/20 cm around leg and foot

Leg is 13"/33 cm to bottom of heel

Foot is 9.5"/24 cm from back of heel to toe

To fit an average to large woman's foot. See Making Socks to Fit You on page 17 for how to customize the fit to any size.

Yarn

Lion Brand Sock Ease, super fine #1 weight yarn (75% wool, 25% nylon; 438 yd./400 m per 3.5 oz./100 g skein)

• 1 skein #178 Snow Cone (Color A)

• 1 skein #174 Apple Green (Color B)

Needles and Other Materials

• US 1 (2.25 mm) set of 4 double-pointed knitting needles

Adjust needle size as necessary to obtain gauge.

Gauge

32 sts x 40 rnds in Boxy Stripe pattern = 4"/10 cm square

Pattern Stitch

Boxy Stripe

Rnds 1–3: With A, knit.

Rnd 4: With B, knit.

Rnd 5: With B, purl.

Rnds 6–7: With A, *Sl 1, k2. Repeat from * around.

Rnds 8–9: Repeat Rnds 4–5.

Repeat Rnds 1–9 for pattern.

A note on the stitch pattern: The pattern is worked with purl stitches throughout the leg and on the top of the foot, but is knit throughout on the bottom of the foot. If preferred you can knit throughout, or just on the top and bottom of the foot for a smoother look and feel.

Leg

With B, CO 64 stitches.

Work in k1, p1 ribbing for 1.5"/3.5 cm.

Begin Boxy Stripe pattern, dec 1 st in the first rnd only—63 sts.

Continue in pattern until sock is approximately 8"/20 cm long, ending at the end of a pattern repeat.

Heel

Heel is worked back and forth in rows in Color B.

Arrange 32 sts on one needle to work the heel.

Row 1: *Sl 1, k1. Repeat from * across.

Row 2: Sl 1, purl across.

Repeat Rows 1–2 until heel flap is roughly square, ending with Row 2.

Row 3: Sl 1, k17, ssk, k1, wrap and turn.

Row 4: Sl l 1, p5, p2tog, p1, wrap and turn.

Row 5: Sl 1, k6, ssk, k1, wrap and turn.

Row 6: Sl 1, p7, p2tog, p1, wrap and turn.

Row 7: Sl 1, k8, ssk, k1, wrap and turn.
Row 8: Sl 1, p9, p2tog, p1, wrap and turn.
Row 9: Sl 1, k10, ssk, k1, wrap and turn.
Row 10: Sl 1, p11, p2tog, p1, wrap and turn.
Row 11: Sl 1, k12, ssk, k1, wrap and turn.
Row 12: Sl 1, p13, p2tog, p1, wrap and turn.
Row 13: Sl 1, k14, ssk, k1, wrap and turn.
Row 14: Sl 1, p15, p2tog, p1, wrap and turn.
Row 15: Sl 1, k16, ssk.
Row 16: Sl 1, p16, p2tog—18 sts rem.

Gusset

Knit across heel stitches, then pick up and knit 23 sts along the side of the heel flap. Work across the leg stitches, and with a new needle, pick up and knit 23 sts on the other side of the heel flap—95 sts. The end of the round will now be here at the side of the heel. Arrange sts so the heel sts are divided onto 2 needles (needles 1 and 3) and the sts that weren't worked during the heel shaping are on 1 needle (needle 2).

Note: Maintain the stitch pattern as much as possible when working decreases. On rounds where the decreases happen in a slip-stitch round, work the decrease within the Color A stitches that are closest to the end of the needle.

Next rnd: Reattach Color A and knit to 3 sts to end of needle 1, k2tog, k1. Work across needle 2, then k1, ssk, and knit to end of needle 3.

Next rnd: Knit.

Next rnd: Continue in Boxy Stripe pattern (starting with Rnd 4), continuing to dec every other row as established. On the bottom of the foot (and top if desired), work all sts as knit sts.

Continue in this manner until 63 sts rem.

Foot

Continue straight in stitch pattern until foot measures 7.5"/19 cm from the back of the heel (or 2"/5 cm from desired length).

Next rnd: Work to last 3 sts of needle 1, k2tog, k1. On needle 2, ssk, k1, work to 3 sts from end, k2tog, k1. For needle 3, k1, ssk, work to end.

Next rnd: Knit.

Repeat these 2 rnds, still maintaining the stitch pattern, until 51 sts rem, ending with a solid round in Color B.

Continue in Color B and St st for the rest of the toe shaping. Dec every other round as established until 31 sts rem, then dec every rnd until 13 sts rem. Dec 1 more st on this last round (I did mine on the bottom of the foot) so that 12 sts rem.

Divide evenly onto 2 needles. Cut yarn, leaving a long tail and graft the toe closed (see page 98 for step-by-step instructions on grafting).

Weave in ends.

Knit the second sock in the same manner.

Slip-Stitch Tweed Top

I have to say, I really love this sweater. The tweed pattern has sort of a houndstooth look and it's really easy to knit.

You could use one color for the "stripes" or choose three related colors as I did. I love the way the pinks work with the green background color and make the green look a little different depending on which pink is near it. That's a great color lesson right there!

This sweater is meant to fit a little more snugly than some of the other garments in this book, but feel free to work a size up if you'd rather have a little more room.

Finished Measurements

32 (34, 36, 38, 40)"/81.25 (87, 91.5, 97, 101.5) cm around chest
20.75 (21.25, 22.25, 22.5, 22.75)"/52.5 (54, 56.5, 57, 57.5) cm
    long
To fit a 34 (36, 38, 40, 42)"/ 87 (91.5, 97, 101.5, 106.75) cm chest.

Yarn

Brown Sheep Company Lamb's Pride Worsted, medium
    weight #4 yarn (85% wool, 15% mohair; 190 yd./174 m
    per 4 oz./113 g skein)
- 2 (2, 2, 3, 3) skeins M-18 Khaki (Color A)
- 1 skein M-34 Victorian Pink (Color B)
- 1 skein M-183 Rosado Rose (Color C)
- 1 skein M-38 Lotus Pink (Color D)

Needles and Other Materials

- US 6 (4 mm) circular knitting needle, 30 to 36"/80 to 90
    cm long cable
- US 7 (4.5 mm) circular knitting needle, 30 to 36"/80 to 90
    cm long cable
- US 6 (4 mm) set of 4 double-pointed knitting needles
- US 7 (4.5 mm) set of 4 double-pointed knitting needles
- Stitch holder or length of waste yarn
- 5 stitch markers, 2 each of the same color, plus 1 addi-
    tional marker of any color
Adjust needle sizes as necessary to obtain gauge.

Gauge

22 sts x 24 rnds in Tweed Stitch with US 7 needles = 4"/10
    cm square

Notes

- The sweater is worked in the round from the bottom up,
    then separated at the shoulders and worked separately.

Sew the shoulder seams, then pick up and knit the
sleeves down from the body. It's a fun construction technique that leaves very little finishing.

Pattern Stitch

Tweed Stitch In the Round

Rnd 1: With contrasting color, *sl 1, k1. Repeat from *
    around.
Rnd 2: With contrasting color, knit.
Rnd 3: With A, *k1, sl 1. Repeat from * around.
Rnd 4: With A, knit.

Tweed Stitch Worked Flat

Row 1: With contrasting color, *sl 1, k1. Repeat from * across.
Row 2: With contrasting color, purl.
Row 3: With A, *k1, sl 1. Repeat from * around.
Row 4: With A, purl.

This is what the slip stitch pattern looks like on the inside of the sweater.

Finished Measurements

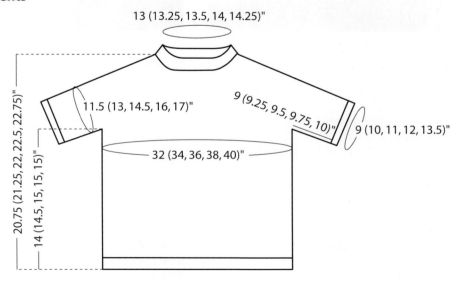

13 (13.25, 13.5, 14, 14.25)"

11.5 (13, 14.5, 16, 17)"

9 (9.25, 9.5, 9.75, 10)"

9 (10, 11, 12, 13.5)"

32 (34, 36, 38, 40)"

20.75 (21.25, 22, 22.5, 22.75)"

14 (14.5, 15, 15, 15)"

Front

Body

With Color A and smaller circular needle, CO 176 (188, 198, 210, 220) sts.

Join to work in the round, being careful not to twist sts.

Work in k1, p1 ribbing for 2"/5 cm.

Change to larger needle and knit 1 rnd in Color A.

Begin Tweed St pattern, with Color B as contrast color.

Work Tweed St pattern 5 times with Color B as contrast color.

Change to Color C as the contrast color and work Tweed St pattern 5 times.

Change to Color D as the contrast color and work Tweed St pattern 5 times.

Continue in this manner until piece measures 14 (14.5, 15, 15, 15)"/35.5 (37, 38, 38, 38) cm, ending with a WS row.

Back

Place 88 (94, 99, 105, 110) sts for front on stitch holder. Work the back of the sweater back and forth in rows across the remaining 88 (94, 99, 105, 110) sts, beginning with the armhole shaping.

ARMHOLE SHAPING

Rows 1–2: Working in pattern, BO 4 sts, work to end of row.
Row 3: BO 2 sts, knit across.
Row 4: BO 2 sts, purl across.
Row 5: Repeat Row 3.
Row 6: Repeat Row 4.
Row 7: K1, ssk, work to last 3 sts, k2tog, k1.
Row 8: Purl.
Row 9: Repeat Row 7—68 (74, 79, 85, 90) sts.

Continue in pattern, working even, until armhole measures 6 (6.25, 6.5, 6.75, 7)"/15 (16, 16.5, 17, 18) cm, ending with a WS row.

NECKLINE SHAPING

Rows 1–2: BO 8 sts, work to end in pattern.
Rows 3–4: BO 6 sts, work to end in pattern.
BO rem 40 (46, 51, 57, 62) sts.

Front

Place the 88 (94, 99, 105, 110) sts for the front on needles and rejoin yarn. Work the front of the sweater back and forth in rows, beginning with the armhole shaping.

ARMHOLE SHAPING

Work the armhole shaping as for the back, then work even until piece measures 4 (4.5, 4.75, 5, 5)"/10 (11.5, 12, 13, 13) cm from where you rejoined the yarn.

NECKLINE SHAPING

On next RS row, work 26 (28, 30, 32, 34) sts, BO 16 (18, 19, 21, 22) sts, work to end. Work just this side of the neck.
BO 3 sts at neck edge 2 times.
Work even until 6 (6.5, 6.75, 7, 7)"/15 (16, 16.5, 17, 18) cm from join.
Next RS row: BO 8 sts at neck edge.
Next RS row: BO 6 sts at neck edge.
BO rem 6 (8, 10, 12, 14) sts.
Join yarn to other side of neck to work a WS row.
BO 3 sts at neck edge 2 times.
Work even until 6 (6.5, 6.75, 7, 7)"/15 (16, 16.5, 17, 18) cm from join.

(continued)

Next WS row: BO 8 sts at neck edge.
Next WS row: BO 6 sts at neck edge.
BO rem 6 (8, 10, 12, 14) sts.
Sew shoulder seams together before knitting sleeves.

Sleeves

Starting at the bottom center of the underarm and with
larger DPNs and Color A, pick up and knit 64 (72, 80, 88,
96) sts evenly around armhole. Place markers after 8 (10,
12, 14, 16) sts (first color), 13 (14, 15, 16, 17) sts (second
color), 22 (24, 26, 28, 30) sts (second color), 13 (14, 15, 16,
17) sts (first color), 8 (10, 12, 14, 16) sts (end of round, can
be any color).
Work to the second marker in the second color, sm, wrap
and turn.
Repeat (working back to what was the first marker in the
second color when you placed them).
Work to the wrapped st, work it along with its wrap, work 1
st, wrap and turn.
Repeat this row until you reach the first color markers. End
on a WS row.
Begin to work in the round, removing markers (other than
the end of round marker) as you come to them and
working wrapped sts together with their wraps.
Work 3 (4, 5, 6, 7) rnds.

Next rnd: K1, k2tog, k to last 3 sts, ssk, k1.
Next 2 rnds: Knit.
Repeat these 3 rnds until 50 (56, 62, 68, 74) sts rem.
Work even until sleeve measures 8 (8.25, 8.5, 8.75, 9)"/20
(21, 21.5, 22, 23) cm from top of the shoulder.
Change to smaller needles and work k1, p1 ribbing for
1"/2.5 cm.
BO in pattern.
Work second sleeve in the same manner.

Finishing

NECKLINE

Using smaller DPNs and Color A and starting at right shoul-
der, pick up and knit 71 (73, 75, 77, 79) sts evenly around
neckline (making sure you have an odd number).
Work 3 rnds in k1, p1 ribbing.
BO loosely in pattern.
Weave in ends.

All About Stranded Knitting

Stranded knitting developed in different parts of the world in slightly different ways. Most people are familiar with Fair Isle knitting, which was developed on one of the Shetland Islands off the coast of Scotland. Fair Isle is sometimes used as a generic term to refer to all color knitting produced by stranding yarn across the back of the work, but it really refers to a specific style that uses particular motifs and colors to form its designs. In traditional Fair Isle knitting you typically don't see one color used for more than five stitches at a time before changing to the other color, though the number of stitches it's acceptable to work in one color before switching varies among stranded knitting traditions.

Stranded knitting is the form of color knitting that looks the most difficult, but the good news is once you get the hang of it, it isn't that hard at all. You are working with two different colors of yarn in the same row or round, so you will have to practice a bit to determine what style of yarn management works best for you.

Three Ways to Manage Yarn in Stranded Knitting

THE PICK AND DROP METHOD

The easiest way to get started with stranded knitting is to hold one strand of yarn in your usual fashion, work the stitches required in that color, drop that yarn, pick up the other one, work those stitches, drop that yarn, and so on.

This is a really slow process and can lead to some pretty funky tension, so it's not really the best choice, but it will get you started. I wouldn't use this method on a big project, though, or you'll drive yourself crazy with all the yarn switching.

When working a stranded knitting pattern, you can simply drop the yarn you are not using, pick up the other color from underneath, and begin knitting with the new color.

TWO YARNS, ONE HAND

Another option is to hold both of the yarns in the same hand you normally use to knit. Some people tension the yarns around different fingers, while others use the same finger and just move it forward or backward depending on which yarn they need to catch.

This is a good method to learn if you're really dominant in one hand or don't want to learn to hold yarn in your other hand for whatever reason.

You can hold both yarns in the same hand you normally would hold your working yarn, only catching the yarn you need for the stitch you are working.

TWO YARNS, TWO HANDS

The way I typically work with two yarns is to hold one in each hand. Usually I work with the main color in my right hand and the contrast color in my left hand, but that's just my preference because I'm more comfortable with English-style knitting.

When I need the main color I work English style; when I need the contrast color I work Continental. It's really easy to switch back and forth if you're comfortable with both styles of knitting. If you're not, practice first by knitting a solid-color swatch in whichever method you don't typically use, then work a two-color swatch to get used to how that feels before you start a big project. I find this method to be very efficient, and as long as I pick up the same yarn in each hand when I work it produces great results. To learn either style of knitting, do a quick YouTube search and you'll find plenty of videos showing you how.

A very efficient method of stranding is to hold one yarn in each hand, working one color English style and the other Continental.

Keeping Good Tension

The most important thing when it comes to working a stranded knitting project is keeping a good tension on the yarns. Because you're carrying the unused yarn across the back of the work, it's really easy to pull too tightly when you form the next stitch in a new color, which will cause the work to pucker.

On the other hand, it's possible to make your floats too loose, which may cause your fingers to catch on them when putting on a sweater or mitts. It takes some practice to get your tension just right, which is another reason swatching comes in handy.

Stretching out the stitches/loops on the right needle before you change colors is one great way to make sure your float is sufficient to not pucker the fabric. You'll have to do this consciously for a while, but with practice it will come naturally and your knitting will look nice and even.

It is important to keep your floats at an even tension with the rest of your knitting, not so tight that they cause your piece to pucker and not so loose that things will get caught on them easily.

Reading a Stranded Knitting Chart

Stranded knitting patterns are usually small motifs of a few stitches that repeat across the work. This is illustrated in the knitting pattern through the use of a chart. The chart will show the part of the pattern that repeats as well as any edge stitches that might be different at the beginning or end of the row or round.

Stranded knitting is typically worked in the round so that you can always see how the pattern is working on the right side. In that case, the knitting chart is always worked from right to left, just as the round of knitting is. Should you have a stranded knitting pattern that is worked flat, the right side rows of the chart are worked from right to left and the wrong side rows are worked from left to right.

Pros of Stranded Knitting

- It makes a really warm fabric in the stranded sections.
- It's an easy way to add small-scale colorwork to a project.
- Charts usually repeat across a project, making it easy to read your knitting and memorize what comes next.

Cons of Stranded Knitting

- Yarn control can be difficult, especially if you're not comfortable working by holding yarn in both hands.
- Keeping an even tension throughout a project is essential: too tight and it will pucker, too loose and the back of your work will be a mess.
- It works best with really small designs and short sections between color changes.

Yarn Dominance in Stranded Knitting

Which yarn you hold in each hand does make a difference when it comes to how your knitting looks in the end. The yarn that comes from underneath the other yarn when you form stitches tends to stand out a little bit more. The technical reason is because that yarn travels farther to get to the needle, so it uses more yarn and thus makes bigger stitches.

It usually isn't a big deal which yarn you hold in which hand, but do be consistent across a project or it may come out looking a little strange in a way you can't quite put your finger on.

How to Make a Stranded Knit Project Your Own

The easiest way to alter a project worked in stranded knitting, of course, is to change the color. Make the color choices bolder or more harmonious and you'll see a big difference in the finished piece.

One great thing about stranded knitting projects is that they usually involve relatively short pattern repeats, so you can easily change out a motif in a project for one you prefer, so long as it uses the same number of stitches. You can draw your own repeating motifs on graph paper if you like, or look to a book full of motifs to find ones you like better than those used in the pattern. (I did some of both for this book, and you'll find a couple of great pattern collections in the Further Reading section at the back of the book.)

You can also add stripes or other colorwork to any solid sections of a project, such as on the body of the Diamond Circular Yoke Sweater.

Bluebird Cowl

This cowl is an easy combination of stripes and stranded colorwork that uses lots of different colors to make a big statement on a small scale. This is not a strictly traditional Fair Isle style pattern, because the floats between colors in the bluebird section can get quite long. Every few stitches, catch the non-working yarn behind the working yarn so the floats don't get too unwieldy.

The yarn I chose, Color by Kristin, is designed by color pro Kristin Nicholas, and all of the colors work really well together, so you can pick any colors you like to make your designs. I particularly like the orange as a background color playing against the cool blue and green of the patterns, and the bright purple is a lot of fun, too.

To change up this cowl, it is easy to substitute bands of any sort of pattern you like to make a colorful and cozy cowl perfect for winter weather.

Finished Measurements

22.5"/57 cm around

13"/33 cm long at longest point of edging

Yarn

Classic Elite Yarn Color by Kristin, worsted/medium weight
#4 yarn (50% wool, 25% alpaca, 25% mohair; 93 yd./85 m
per 1.7 oz./50 g ball)

- 1 ball #3232 Raspberry (Color A)
- 1 ball #3244 Caramel (Color B)
- 1 ball #3258 Geranium (Color C)
- 1 ball #3278 October Leaves (Color D)
- 1 ball #3215 Spring Green (Color E)
- 1 ball #3257 Cornflower (Color F)

Needles and Other Materials

- US 7 (4.5 mm) 16 in./40 cm long circular knitting needle

Adjust needle size as necessary to obtain gauge.

Gauge

16 sts x 21 rnds in St st in the round = 4"/10 cm square

Edging

Using Color A, CO 5 sts.

Row 1: Sl 1, k1, yo twice, k2tog, k1.

Row 2: Sl 1, k2, p1, k2.

Row 3: Sl 1, k3, yo twice, k2.

Row 4: Sl 1, k2, p1, k4.

Row 5: Sl 1, k1, yo twice, k2tog, k4.

Row 6: Sl 1, k5, p1, k2.

Row 7: Sl 1, k8.

Row 8: BO 4, k4.

Repeat these 8 rows until piece measures 26"/66 cm. BO
rem sts.

Sew the cast on and bound off edges together to make the
edging into a loop.

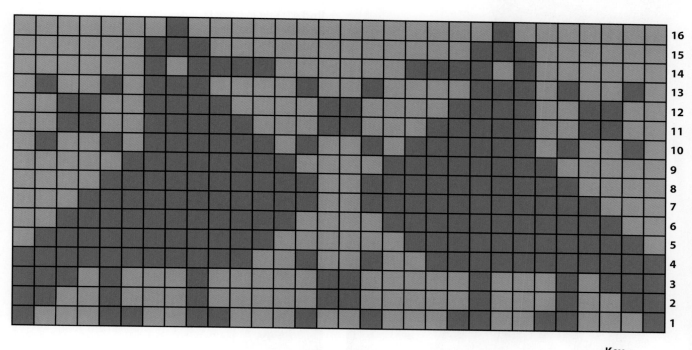

Bluebird Chart

Key

Color D

Color F

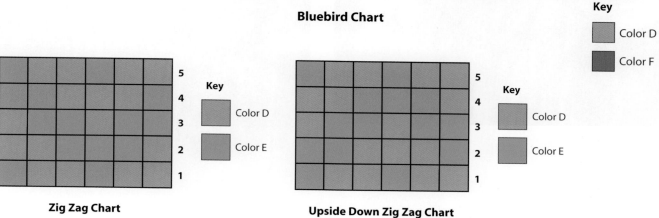

Zig Zag Chart

Key

Color D

Color E

Upside Down Zig Zag Chart

Key

Color D

Color E

Cowl

Using Color B, pick up and knit 90 sts along the slip-stitch edge. Begin working in the round.

Rnds 1–2: Knit.

Rnd 3: Knit in Color C.

Rnds 4–6: Knit in Color B.

Rnd 7: Knit in Color C.

Rnd 8: Knit in Color D.

Rnds 9–13: Work Zigzag Chart in Colors D and E.

Rnd 14: Knit in Color D.

Rnd 15: Knit in Color C.

Rnds 16–18: Knit in Color B.

Rnd 19: Knit in Color C.

Rnd 20: Knit in Color D.

Rnd 21: Knit in Color F.

Rnd 22: Knit in Color D.

Rnds 23–38: Work Bluebird Chart in Colors D and F.

Rnd 39: Knit in Color D.

Rnd 40: Knit in Color F.

Rnd 41: Knit in Color D.

Rnd 42: Knit in Color C.

Rnds 43–45: Knit in Color B.

Rnd 46: Knit in Color C.

Rnd 47: Knit in Color D.

Rnds 48–52: Work Upside Down Zigzag Chart in Colors D
  and E.
Rnd 53: Knit in Color D.
Rnd 54: Knit in Color C.
Rnds 55–57: Knit in Color B.
Rnd 58: Knit in Color C.
Rnds 59–61: Knit in Color B.
Rnd 62: Knit in Color A.
BO.
Weave in ends.

Two-Color Cable Hat

Working a simple cable in two colors looks a lot more complex than it is. You simply work one part of the cable in one color and the rest in the other, just as with any other stranded knitting project. Alternating stitches of each color fill in the spaces between the cables, making this an easy, quick, and colorful project.

Work it in team colors and you'll be warm for every game, or choose your two favorite colors for this funky warmer.

Finished Measurements

20"/51 cm around
9"/23 cm long
To fit an average woman.

Yarn

SWTC Saphira, bulky weight #5 yarn (100% superwash
 wool; 131 yd./120 m per 3.5 oz./100 g skein)
- 1 skein #606 Blue (Color A)
- 1 skein #579 Yellow (Color B)

Needles and Other Materials

- US 10 (6 mm) 16"/40 cm long circular needle
- US 10 (6 mm) set of 4 double-pointed needles
- Cable needle or spare DPN (same size as your working
 needle or smaller)

Adjust needle size as necessary to obtain gauge.

Gauge

18 sts x 18 rnds in alternating two-color pattern = 4"/10 cm
 square

Pattern Stitch

Alternating Stockinette

Pattern row: *K1 in Color A, k1 in Color B. Repeat from *
 across.

Brim

Using the circular needle and Color A, CO 96 sts. Join to
 work in the round, being careful not to twist sts.
Rnd 1: *K3 in Color A, p3 in Color B. Repeat from * around.
Repeat Rnd 1 for 2"/5 cm.
Next rnd: *K3 in Color A, k3 in Color B, then alternating colors every other stitch, k1, M1, k2, M1, k2, M1, k1. Repeat
 from * around—120 sts.

Cables and Decreases

Cable rnd: *Slip 3 sts onto cable needle and hold in front,
 k3, then k3 from cable needle, keeping all in original colors. Work next 9 sts in opposite color from previous rnd.
 Repeat from * around.
Work 3 rnds knitting the cable sts in same color and alter-
 nating colors in other sts, and work the cable cross each
 fourth round.
Continue in this manner until hat measures 6"/15 cm.
Note: Change to DPNs when circular becomes difficult to use.
Dec rnd: Dec 1 st at each end of each of the alternating
 color sections, continuing to change colors as estab-
 lished and keeping the colors alternating as much as
 possible throughout the dec section—104 sts.
Next rnd: Knit.
Next rnd: Repeat Dec rnd—88 sts.
Next rnd: Repeat Cable rnd.
Next rnd: Repeat dec rnd—72 sts.

Next rnd: Knit.
Next rnd: Keeping cable sts as usual, work a k2tog, k1 in
 rem spacer sts—64 sts.
Next rnd: Repeat Cable rnd.
From here on, alternate every stitch of every rnd as much as
 possible.
Next rnd: *K6, k2tog. Repeat from * around—56 sts.
Next rnd: *K5, k2tog. Repeat from * around—48 sts.
Next rnd: *K4, k2tog. Repeat from * around—40 sts.

(continued)

Next rnd: *K3, k2tog. Repeat from * around—32 sts.
Next rnd: *K2, k2tog. Repeat from * around—24 sts.
Next rnd: *K1, k2tog. Repeat from * around—16 sts.
Next rnd: *K2tog. Repeat from * around—8 sts.
Cut yarn, leaving a long tail. Place yarn on yarn needle, slip
    sts onto needle and pull yarn tight to close up the top of
    the hat. Weave in ends.

Checkerboard Mittens

A lot of knitting projects use bold colors, but it's also fun to combine one great color with a basic, go-with-almost-anything color like white or black. In this case I went with a classic combination of red and black for an easy-to-knit pair of mittens reminiscent of a checkerboard. This project is a great introduction to stranded knitting because you don't have to follow a chart or really even think much about what you're doing. I also love the alternating color thumbs, which are really cute and practical from a knitting standpoint, keeping the yarn moving around without long floats.

Finished Measurements

9.5"/24 cm long
7"/18 cm around hand
To fit an average woman.

Yarn

Valley Yarns Northfield, medium weight #4 yarn (70% merino wool, 20% baby alpaca, 10% silk; 124 yd./113 m per 1.7 oz./50 g ball)

- 1 ball Red (Color A)
- 1 ball Black (Color B)

Needles and Other Materials

- US 6 (4 mm) set of 4 double-pointed knitting needles
- 2 stitch markers
- Stitch holder

Adjust needle size as necessary to obtain gauge.

Gauge

24 sts x 24 rnds in Checkerboard Pattern, slightly stretched = 4"/10 cm square
22 sts in ribbing = 4"/10 cm

Pattern Stitches

Corrugated Ribbing

Pattern row: *K1 in Color A, p1 in Color B. Repeat from * around.

Checkerboard Pattern

Rnds 1–4: *K4 in Color A, k4 in Color B. Repeat from * across.
Rnds 5–8: *K4 in Color B, k4 in Color A. Repeat from * across.
Repeat Rnds 1–8 for pattern.

Mitt

Holding both colors together, CO 40 stitches.

Work into CO row, treating the two yarns as one (i.e., each 2 loops CO together as a single stitch), and work k1 in Color A, p1 in Color B around for 2"/5 cm—40 sts.

Next rnd: *K4 in Color A, k4 in Color B. Repeat from * for 20 sts total. Place marker, CO 1 in Color A (I used backward loop), pm, continue in Checkerboard Pattern as established to end of round.

Inc rnd: Keep in pattern across body of mitten to first marker, sm, M1, **knit alternating colors to second marker**, M1, sm, work to end of rnd maintaining Checkerboard pattern.

Work Inc rnd as established every 3 rnds 6 more times—15 total thumb sts.

Place these sts on a holder.

Knit hand in Checkerboard pattern to 5.5"/14 cm.

SHAPING THE TIP

Next rnd: Ssk, k16, k2tog, ssk, k to 2 sts from end, k2tog. As you work through the shaping, work sts in whatever color makes the most sense to you.

Next rnd: Knit.

Dec as established every other rnd until 24 sts rem.

Dec every rnd until 8 sts rem.

Cut yarn, thread one color onto yarn needle, slip sts onto yarn and pull tight.

Weave in end.

THUMB

Place held sts on needles and join yarn to work across. Pick up and knit 3 sts along the mitten side—18 sts.

Knit, continuing to change colors every stitch, for 1.5"/4 cm from the join.

Next rnd: *K4, k2tog. Repeat from * around—15 sts.

Next rnd: Knit.

Next rnd: *K3, k2tog. Repeat from * around—12 sts.

Next rnd: Knit.

Next rnd: *K2, k2tog. Repeat from * around—9 sts.

Next rnd: *K1, k2tog. Repeat from * around—6 sts.

Cut yarn, thread one color onto yarn needle, slip sts onto yarn and pull tight. Weave in ends.

Knit second mitten in the same manner.

Wear Your Heart on Your Socks

Hearts are a classic graphic pattern, and I knew I wanted to include some hearts in this book. These socks are fun to knit, and I like that the yarn I used isn't completely solid so there's some variation in color throughout.

I'm a big fan of gray with a bright color, but you can use any neutral (and, indeed, any color for the hearts) that you like to suit your style.

These socks are worked from the top down with a short-row heel and with patterning all over except on the cuff, heel, and toe. This makes the socks super warm and cozy, and also helps them stay up.

Finished Measurements

8.5"/22 cm around

9"/23 cm long from cuff to bottom of heel

Foot is 9.5"/24 cm from back of heel to toe

To fit an average-sized woman's foot. See Making Socks to Fit You on page 17 for how to customize the fit to any size.

Yarn

Blue Moon Fiber Arts Socks that Rock, super fine #1 weight yarn (100% superwash merino; 405 yd./370 m per 5.5 oz./156 g skein)

- 1 skein Deep Unrelenting Grey (Color A)
- 1 skein Boysenberry (Color B)

Needles and Other Materials

- US 1 (2.5 mm) set of 4 double-pointed knitting needles

Adjust needle size as necessary to obtain gauge.

Gauge

34 sts x 39 rnds in Heart pattern = 4"/10 cm square

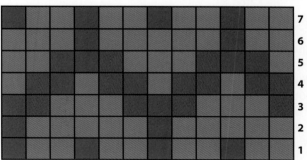

Heart Chart

Key

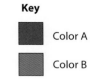

Color A

Color B

Leg

Using Color A, CO 72 sts. Divide onto 3 needles and join in round, being careful not to twist sts.

Work in k2, p2 ribbing for 1.5"/4 cm.

Knit 2 rnds.

Begin to work Heart Chart, working 2 rnds in Color A between each repeat.

Work full chart 6 times.

After last repeat, knit 1 rnd in Color A.

Shown with Polka Dot Socks

Turning the Heel

The heel is worked back and forth on 36 sts in Color A.
Row 1: Knit to 1 st from end of heel section, wrap and turn.
Row 2: Purl to 1 st from end of heel section, wrap and turn.
Row 3: Knit to 1 st before previous wrap, wrap and turn.
Row 4: Purl to 1 st before previous wrap, wrap and turn.
Continue in this manner, working 1 fewer st each row, until 10 sts are unworked in the middle.
Work to first wrapped st, work the st along with its wrap, wrap and turn. This st now has 2 wraps.
Continue across, working the first wrapped stitch on each row and wrapping sts again as you come to them until all sts in heel have been worked. When you get to the end of the heel sts, wrap the first st on either end of the leg sts.

Foot

Begin to work in the round again, working wraps as you come to them. Arrange sts so that the top of the foot is on one needle (needle 1) and the bottom of the foot is divided onto two needles (needles 2 and 3). Side of the foot is still the end of the round.
Work chart five more times, again working 2 rnds in Color A between each chart repeat.
Knit 1 rnd in Color A.

Toe

Toe is worked in Color A.
Rnd 1: Needle 1: K1, ssk, k to 3 sts from end of needle, k2tog, k1.
　　　　Needle 2: K1, ssk, k to end.
　　　　Needle 3: K to 3 sts from end, k2tog, k1.
Rnd 2: Knit.
Repeat Rnds 1–2 until 40 sts rem.
Work Rnd 1 every round until 16 sts rem.
Cut yarn, leaving a long tail. Arrange sts onto two needles and graft the toe closed (see page 98 for step-by-step instructions on how to graft).
Weave in ends.
Knit the second sock in the same manner.

Diamond Circular Yoke Sweater

The circular yoke sweater is a classic from Iceland, and I made mine in Icelandic wool, which makes for an extra warm and cozy sweater. The increasingly larger diamond motifs fit nicely around the yoke, where increases are worked over just a few rounds (in contrast to the raglan design, where increases are made every other round). For a more dramatic look, use a non-neutral color for the background. Maybe red or blue?

This sweater just begs to be worn on the coldest days of winter, playing in the snow with the kids or on a ski trip. Meant to be worn with layers underneath, the size is roomy. Check the finished measurements and consider how much ease you want when choosing your size. I know I'm going to get a lot of use out of mine, because I'm always cold!

Finished Measurements

39 (40, 42, 44.5, 46)"/99 (102, 107, 113, 117) cm around chest
To fit a 32 (34, 36, 38, 40)"/81 (86, 91.5, 101.5) cm chest.

Yarn

Alafoss Lopi, bulky weight #5 yarn (100% wool; 109 yd./
100 m per 3.5 oz./100 g skein)
- 6 (6, 7, 7, 8) skeins #57 Gray (Color A)
- 1 (1, 1, 1, 2) skein(s) #1236 Burnt Orange (Color B)

Needles and Other Materials

- US 9 (5.5 mm) circular needles, 16"/40 cm and 30"/80 cm
  long cables
- US 10 (6 mm) 30"/80 cm long circular needle
- US 9 (5.5 mm) set of 4 double-pointed needles
- US 10 (6 mm) set of 4 double-pointed needles
- Stitch holders or spare yarn
Adjust needle sizes as necessary to obtain gauge.

Gauge

14 sts x 19 rnds in St st in the round with larger needles =
4"/10 cm square

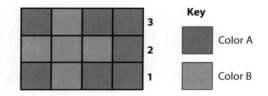

Chart A

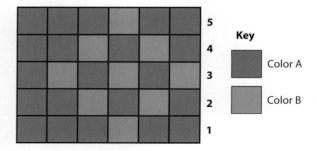

Chart B

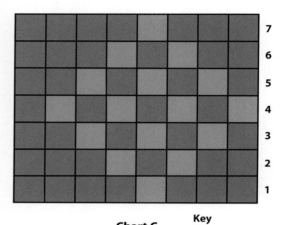

Chart C

Finished Measurements

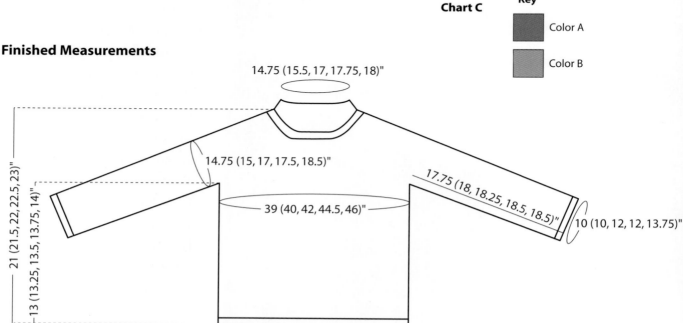

Front

Increase Rounds and Diamond Patterns

With Color B and smaller size 9 circular needle, CO 52 (54, 60, 62, 64) sts and join in round, being careful not to twist the sts.

Rnd 1: Change to Color A and knit.

Rnds 2–5: *K1, p1. Repeat from * around.

Rnd 6: Change to larger needle, and knit.

Rnd 7: *K2, M1. Repeat from * around—78 (81, 90, 93, 96) sts.

Rnd 8, *Sizes 34 and 38 only*: K1, M1, k to 1 st from end, M1, k1.

Rnd 8, *Sizes 36 and 40 only*: K1, M1, k1, M1, k to 1 st from end, M1, k1.

Rnd 8, *Size 42 only*: K1, M1, k1, M1, k to 2 sts from end, M1, k1, M1, K1.

At end of Rnd 8, you will have 80 (84, 92, 96, 100) sts.

Rnds 9–11: Work Chart A.

Here you can see how your stranded pattern should look from the inside of the sweater—nice and neat floats.

Rnd 12: With Color A, knit.
Rnd 13: *K2, M1. Repeat from * around—120 (126, 138, 144, 150) sts.
Rnd 14: Knit.
Rnds 15–19: Work Chart B.
Rnd 20: With Color A, knit.
Rnd 21: *K3, M1. Repeat from * around—160 (168, 184, 192, 200) sts.
Rnd 22: Knit.
Rnds 23–29: Work Chart C.
Rnd 30: With Color A, knit.
Rnd 31: *K4, M1. Repeat from * around—200 (210, 230, 240, 250) sts.
Knit even until yoke measures 8 (8.25, 8.5, 8.75, 9)"/20.25 (21, 21.75, 22.25, 23) cm.
Work next increase row as follows for your size:
Size 34: M1, *k8, M1. Repeat from * around—226 sts.
Size 36: M1, *k10, M1. Repeat from * around—232 sts.
Size 38: M1, *K10, M1. Repeat from * around—254 sts.
Size 40: *K10, M1. Repeat from * around—264 sts.
Size 42: M1, *K10, M1. Repeat from * around—276 sts.

Body

K68 (70, 74, 78, 80). Place 45 (46, 53, 54, 58) sts on stitch holder or spare yarn for sleeve. Repeat on other side.
Knit even for 10 (10.25, 10.5, 10.75, 11)"/25.5 (26, 26.75, 27.5, 28) cm.
Next rnd: Knit, increasing 2 (4, 2, 0, 2) sts—138 (144, 150, 156, 162) sts on needles.
Work Chart B.
Knit 3 rnds.
Change to longer size 9 needle and k1, p1 for 4 rnds.
Change to Color B and BO in knit.

Sleeves

Using larger dpns, place 45 (46, 53, 54, 58) held stitches onto needles. Pick up and knit 7 sts along base of sleeve with Color A—52 (53, 60, 61, 65) sts.
Rnds 1–4: Knit.
Dec rnd: K1, k2tog, k to 3 sts from end, ssk, k1—2 sts dec.
Work Dec rnd every eighth rnd 7 times total—38 (39, 46, 47, 51) sts.
Knit even until sleeve measures 15 (15.25, 15.5, 15.75, 16)"/38 (38.75, 39.5, 40, 40.75) cm from pick up rnd.
Next rnd: Knit, decreasing 2 (3, 4, 5, 3) sts—36 (36, 42, 42, 48) sts.
Work chart B.
Next 3 rnds: Knit in Color A.
Next 4 rnds: Change to size 9 needles and k1, p1 around.
Change to Color B and BO in knit.
Repeat for other sleeve.
Weave in ends.
This sweater benefits from blocking to smooth everything out and to get the ribbing to lie flat.

Intarsia Knitting

ntarsia is the color knitting method to choose when you want to make a big statement with your knitting. Graphic elements like hearts, stars, the state of Texas, or a flower can easily be knit into fabric using this method.

The term intarsia comes from the world of woodworking, where it refers to a pattern inset into wood, much like the picture is inset into a plain background of knitting. An intarsia design can take up a lot more space than a small stranded knitting motif, so it's great when you want to make a single image stand out, as in the flowers on the sweater in this chapter. But you can also use it to great effect on a smaller scale, as shown on the polka-dot socks.

How to Knit Intarsia

When working a pattern in intarsia, you knit across in the main color, then drop that yarn and work stitches in the contrasting color. When finished with that color, drop it and join a new ball of the main color and continue across.

The key to proper yarn management here is that you bring the new color up from underneath the old one, thereby twisting the yarns together and locking the different colors of knitting together. If you don't do that, you'll just be knitting a bunch of separate little pieces of knitting instead of one cohesive fabric.

Always bring the new color up from underneath the old one, twisting the yarns together and locking the different colors of knitting together.

This means, of course, that your yarn is going to get twisted and tangled and turn into a big, horrible mess if you aren't diligent. One thing that helps is using relatively short (an arm's length or two) strands of yarn rather than working from big balls. When you have loose strands at the back of the work, you can untangle them with your fingers as you would messy hair and they stay more manageable. Of course, you'll probably end up with more ends to weave in this way, but there are going to be a lot of yarn ends no matter what.

When you come to the color change, drop the color you are working with and join the new color.

Pros of Intarsia Knitting

- The large scale is great for when you want to make a bold, graphic statement.
- Pieces are generally knit flat, which is good for people intimidated by knitting in the round.
- You can easily swap out an intarsia design you like better if you don't like the one shown in the pattern.
- It's relatively easy because you're only working with one strand of yarn at a time.

To make bold, graphic statements with your knitting, intarsia is the way to go!

Cons of Intarsia Knitting

- It can only easily be knit flat, so garments have to be seamed at the end.
- Lots and lots of ends to weave in.
- Keeping track of many strands of yarn across a row can be a challenge.
- The yarns have to be untangled regularly.
- You have to be able to read a chart and pay attention while you're knitting.
- It can be difficult to get a lot of detail in a design; it's better for simple, bold shapes, unless you want to add a lot of finishing details.

Making an Intarsia Pattern Your Own

As I said in the Pros section above, you can swap out an intarsia design relatively easily. If you have or can draw out another chart that you would like to work instead of a given design, as long as it fits in the space given, you should be able to do the swap.

You'll want to think about how much space the new design takes up and whether you want to center it on the project. Here again, a gauge swatch is your friend because you'll be able to see how many stitches and rows across the new design is and can figure out where you need to place it on your project.

Superstar Scarf

Intarsia works best when you use a nice, simple, graphic image, like this star. It makes a big impact without being difficult to knit.

The yarn I used, Malabrigo Worsted, is supersoft and great to work with. You will love it while you are knitting and you will love it while you are wearing it. This scarf is sure to become a go-to scarf in your collection. It's also perfect for men or women, so keep this one in mind for gift knitting. Work it in rather neutral colors like I did, go bold with school or sports team colors, or try black and hot pink or any other color combination that suits your fancy.

Finished Measurements

5.5"/14 cm wide x 62"/157 cm long, after
blocking

Yarn

1 skein Malabrigo Worsted, worsted/medium
weight #4 yarn (100% wool; 210 yd./192 m
per 3.5 oz./100 g skein)
- 1 skein #507 Pigeon (Color A)
- 1 skein #508 Blue Graphite (Color B)

Needles and Other Materials

- US 9 (5.5 mm) needles
*Adjust needle size as necessary to obtain
gauge.*

Gauge

16 sts x 20 rows in St st = 4"/10 cm square
*Gauge is not that critical, but needs to be tight
enough to not look sloppy.*

Pattern Stitch

Seed Stitch (odd number of sts)
Pattern row: K1, *p1, k1. Repeat from *
across.

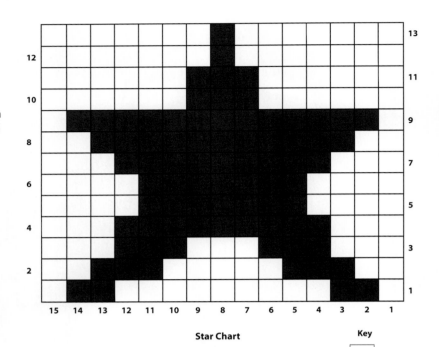

Star Chart

Key

☐ Color A

■ Color B

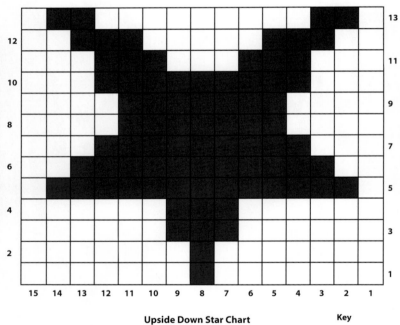

Upside Down Star Chart

Key

☐ Color A

■ Color B

Scarf

With Color A, CO 23.

Work in Seed St for 1"/2.5 cm.

Keeping first and last 4 sts in Seed St, work the remaining 15 sts in St st (knit on RS, purl on WS) for 1"/2.5 cm.

Keeping edges in Seed St and body in St st, work Star Chart.

Work 11 rows (2"/5 cm) in plain St st.

Repeat Star Chart with 11 rows of plain knitting between until piece measures 30"/76 cm after border.

Begin to work Upside Down Star Chart as established for about 29"/71 cm, ending with a chart. I worked a total of 13 stars on my version: 7 right side up and 6 upside down. Feel free to make your scarf a little longer so you can get 7 in each direction if you'd rather.

Work 1"/2.5 cm in St st.

Work 1"/2.5 cm in Seed Stitch.

BO in pattern.

Weave in ends.

Block to help edges lie flat.

Argyle Style Hat

hen I first thought about the projects for this book, I wanted to make my intarsia socks argyle because that's such a classic design. But then I realized that maybe it was a little too classic and that an argyle-style hat, complete with a bold diamond and diagonal lines worked in duplicate stitch, would be a lot more fun.

This hat is slightly slouchy, perfect for people with a lot of hair or who just love the slouchy style.

Finished Measurements

21"/53 cm around
11"/28 cm long
To fit an adult woman in a slouchy style.

Yarn

Harrisville Designs' New England Highland,
  worsted/medium weight #4 yarn (100% wool; 200
  yd./183 m per 3.5 oz./100 g skein)
- 1 skein #55 Pebble (Color A)
- 1 skein #64 Raspberry (Color B)
- 1 skein #6 Cornsilk (Color C)

Needles and Other Materials

- US 7 (4.5 mm) needles
- 2 stitch markers
Adjust needle size as necessary to obtain gauge.

Gauge

19 sts x 29 rows in St st = 4"/10 cm square

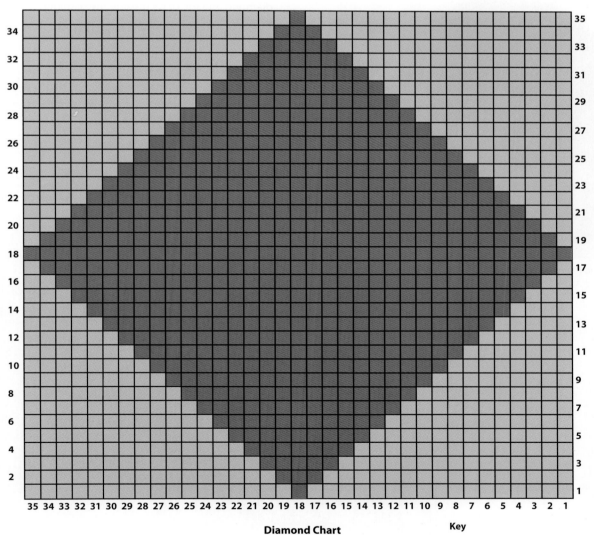

Diamond Chart

Key

Color A   Color B

Hat

Using Color A, CO 102 sts.

Work in k2, p2 ribbing for 1"/2.5 cm.

Work in St st (knit on RS, purl on WS) for 1"/2.5 cm.

Next row: K34, pm for beginning of chart, work Diamond Chart, pm for end of chart, knit rem sts.

Work Diamond Chart as established.

Work in St st for 1"/2.5 cm after chart.

Begin decreasing, purling all WS rows.

Next RS row: K1, *k8, k2tog. Repeat from * to last st, k1— 92 sts.

Next RS row: K1, *k7, k2tog. Repeat from * to last st, k1— 82 sts.

Next RS row: K1, *k6, k2tog. Repeat from * to last st, k1— 72 sts.

Next RS row: K1, *k5, k2tog. Repeat from * to last st, k1— 62 sts.

Next RS row: K1, *k4, k2tog. Repeat from * to last st, k1— 52 sts.

Next RS row: K1, *k3, k2tog. Repeat from * to last st, k1— 42 sts.

Next RS row: K1, *k2, k2tog. Repeat from * to last st, k1— 32 sts.

Next RS row: K1, *k1, k2tog. Repeat from * to last st, k1— 22 sts.

Next RS row: K1, *k2tog. Repeat from * to last st, k1— 12 sts.

Cut yarn, leaving a long tail. Thread yarn onto yarn needle and slip rem sts onto yarn. Pull tight.

Finishing

At this point, you probably want to add the duplicate stitch before seaming, although you can seam first if you prefer. For step-by-step instructions on working duplicate stitch, see page 97. Find the center stitch of the diamond chart and work from there, making diagonal lines of duplicate stitch with Color C radiating in each direction across the diamond and for 10 sts outside the diamond on each side.

Use yarn tail to seam the side of the hat closed with mattress stitch.

Weave in ends.

Intarsia from the wrong side.

Reindeer Games Mittens

ntarsia, perhaps more than any other form of colorwork, provides lots of options for bringing whimsy into your knitting. It makes your knitting into a blank canvas onto which you can knit anything you can dream up.

I wanted these mittens to look like winter, and I also wanted to give a nod to the great knitting traditions of Canada and northern Europe, so I stitched a reindeer on the backs of the mitts.

These mittens are sure to brighten your day, and they are very easy to knit. They're also a really quick project thanks to thicker yarn (I knit these in a weekend).

I love the reindeer in a somewhat non-traditional color, but go ahead and use classic browns, whites, and grays if you'd rather. Or go with red and green for holiday mitts.

Finished Measurements

7.5"/19 cm around palm
9"/23 cm long
To fit an average adult woman.

Yarn

Bernat Vickie Howell Sheep(ish), worsted/medium weight
#4 yarn (70% acrylic, 30% wool; 167 yd./153 m per 3
oz./85 g ball)

- 1 ball #6 Magenta(ish) (Color A)
- 1 ball #3 Grey(ish) (Color B)

Needles and Other Materials

- US 8 (5 mm) needles, or size needed to obtain gauge
- 2 stitch markers
- Stitch holder or waste yarn

Gauge

17 sts x 22 rows in St st = 4"/10 cm square

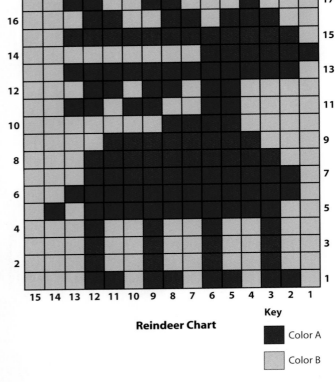

Reindeer Chart

Key

■ Color A
▨ Color B

Right Mitten

Using Color A, CO 30 sts.

Work in k2, p2 ribbing for 3"/7.5 cm, ending on a WS row.

Next row: Change to Color B and k15, pm, M1, k1, M1, pm, k to end, M1—33 sts.

Next row: Purl.

Next row: Work Reindeer Chart across first 15 sts, work gusset sts, knit to end.

Continue working Reindeer Chart and *at the same time* inc 2 sts inside gusset as established every 3 rows 3 times— 9 sts total.

Next row: Work to gusset sts, place those 9 sts on a holder or spare yarn, CO 1 and work across row—31 sts for hand.

Once chart is complete, work in St st until piece measures about 5"/13 cm from top of ribbing.

Begin decreasing, purling every WS row.

Dec 3 sts evenly in the next row—28 sts.

Next RS row: *K5, k2tog. Repeat from * across—24 sts.

Next RS row: *K4, k2tog. Repeat from * across—20 sts.

Next RS row: *K3, k2tog. Repeat from * across—16 sts.

Next RS row: *K2, k2tog. Repeat from * across—12 sts.

Next RS row: *K1, k2tog. Repeat from * across—8 sts.

Cut yarn, leaving a long tail for seaming. Place yarn on yarn needle and slip sts onto yarn, pulling tight.

Use yarn to work mattress stitch to seam up the side of the hand (you can do this before or after you work the thumb, whichever you prefer).

THUMB

Place 9 held sts on needle and CO 1—10 sts.

Work in St st until thumb measures 2"/5 cm from where sts were picked up.

Next RS row: *K1, k2tog. Repeat from * across, ending k1— 7 sts.

Next row: Purl.

Next row: *K2tog. Repeat from * across—4 sts.

Cut yarn, leaving a long tail for seaming. Place yarn on yarn needle and slip sts onto yarn, pulling tight.

Use yarn to work mattress stitch to seam side of thumb.

Weave in remaining ends.

Left Mitten

Work as for right mitten, but begin the Reindeer Chart once you pass the thumb gusset sts.

Polka Dot Socks

Once I decided I didn't want to make my socks with an argyle design, I had to come up with something else, and I finally settled on polka dots. I also decided to only put the dots on the leg of the sock so that I could work the heel and the join in the round for the foot, meaning there would not be an uncomfortable seam in the shoe.

I worked the foot in plain green, but an interesting alternative that would still not cause a seam would be to work the foot in stripes. Now those would be some eye-catching socks!

I love the play of the cool silvery gray against the bright green, but just about any color combination you like would be great in these funky socks.

Finished Measurements

7.25"/18 cm around the leg and foot
9"/23 cm long from top of leg to bottom of heel
8.5"/21.5 cm long from the back of the heel to the
    end of the toe

> *Note: Because of the charted stitches, if you change the stitch count for these socks, you will also need to adapt the chart. An easy way to change the size on a pattern like this without changing stitch count is to use slightly larger needles or thicker yarn to adjust your gauge. With just a slight adjustment to the given gauge, working 27 sts = 4"/10 cm, the leg and foot size of this sock will become 8.25"/21 cm. For more on customizing sock sizes, see page 17.*

Yarn

Knit Picks Stroll, fingering/super fine weight #1
    yarn (75% superwash merino, 25% nylon; 231
    yd./211 m per 1.7 oz./50 g skein)
- 2 skeins #25607 Everglade Heather (Color A)
- 1 skein #25023 Dove Heather (Color B)

To fit an average-sized woman's foot. See Making Socks to Fit You on page 17 for how to customize the fit to any size.

Needles and Other Materials

- US 1 (2.25 mm) set of 4 double-pointed needles
Adjust needle size as necessary to obtain gauge.

Gauge

31 sts x 39 rows in St st worked flat = 4"/10 cm
    square

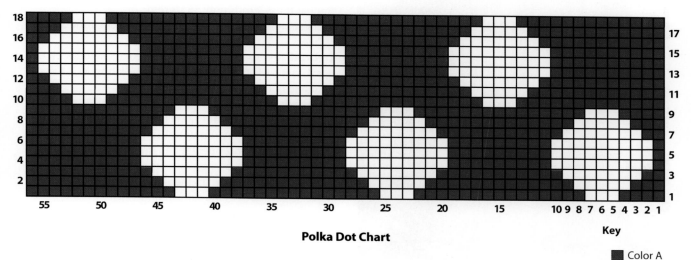

Polka Dot Chart

Key

Color A
Color B

Leg

With Color A, CO 56 sts.
Work in k1, p1 ribbing for 1.5"/3.75 cm.
Work 2 rows in St st, then begin Polka Dot Chart.
Work the full chart twice, then the first 9 rows of the chart
    again (5 rows of dots total).

Heel

The heel is worked back and forth on 28 sts.
Row 1: *Sl 1, k1. Repeat from * across.
Row 2: Sl 1, purl across.
Repeat Rows 1–2 until heel is roughly square, ending on a
    WS row (I worked 32 rows).
Next row: Sl 1, k15, ssk, k1, wrap and turn.
Next row: Sl 1, p5, p2tog, p1, wrap and turn.
Next row: Sl 1, k6, ssk, k1, wrap and turn.
Next row: Sl 1, p7, p2tog, p1, wrap and turn.
Next row: Sl 1, k8, ssk, k1, wrap and turn.
Next row: Sl 1, p9, p2tog, p1, wrap and turn.
Next row: Sl 1, k10, ssk, k1, wrap and turn.
Next row: Sl 1, p11, p2tog, p1, wrap and turn.
Next row: Sl 1, k12, ssk, k1, wrap and turn.
Next row: Sl 1, p13, p2tog, p1, wrap and turn.
Next row: Sl 1, k14, ssk, k1, wrap and turn.
Next row: P across, dec 1 more st—16 sts rem.

Foot

Next RS row: Knit across 16 sts, pick up and knit 16 sts
    along side of heel flap (this is needle 1), knit across held
    leg sts (needle 2), pick up and knit 16 sts along other side
    of heel flap to join in rnd. Knit 8 sts from heel again (nee-
    dle 3). Center of heel is now end of rnd.
Next rnd: Knit to 3 sts from end of needle 1, k2tog, k1. Knit
    across needle 2. K1, ssk, k to end on needle 3.
Next rnd: Knit.
Repeat these 2 rnds until 56 sts rem.
Work straight until foot measures 7.5"/19 cm from back of
    heel.
Dec rnd: Knit to 3 sts from end of needle 1, k2tog, k1. K1,
    ssk, knit to 3 sts from end of needle 2, k2tog, k1. K1, ssk, k
    to end of needle 3.
Next rnd: Knit.
Repeat these 2 rnds until 32 sts rem.
Repeat Dec rnd every rnd until 16 sts rem.
Arrange rem sts on 2 needles and graft the toe closed. See
    page 98 for step-by-step instructions on how to graft.
Weave in ends and sew up the side of the leg.
Make second sock in the same manner.

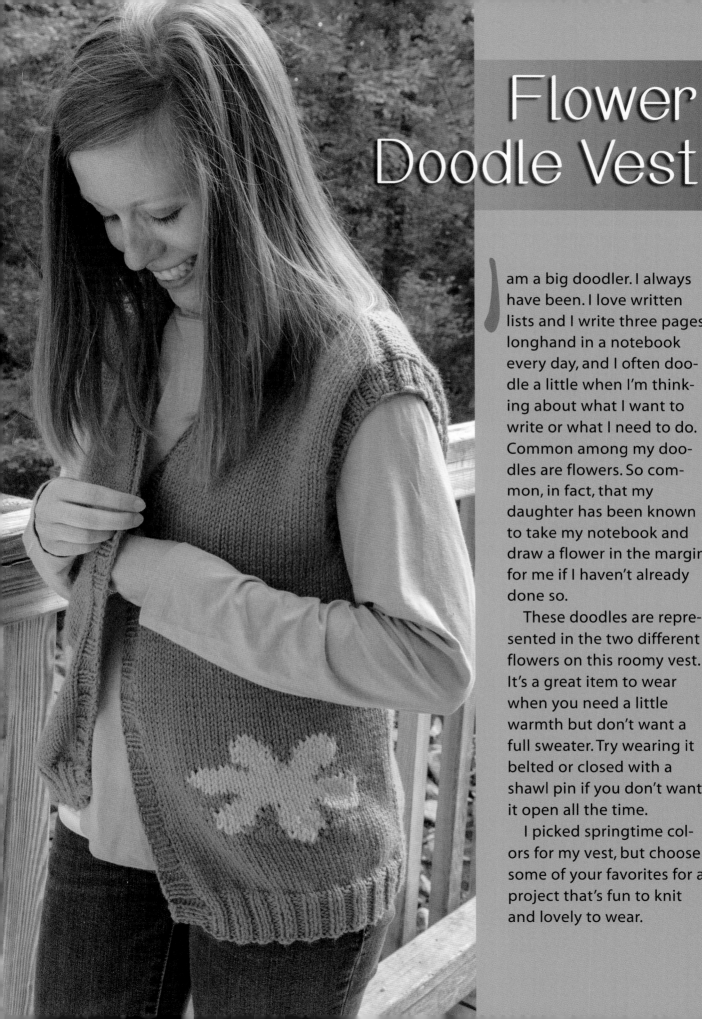

Flower Doodle Vest

I am a big doodler. I always have been. I love written lists and I write three pages longhand in a notebook every day, and I often doodle a little when I'm thinking about what I want to write or what I need to do. Common among my doodles are flowers. So common, in fact, that my daughter has been known to take my notebook and draw a flower in the margin for me if I haven't already done so.

These doodles are represented in the two different flowers on this roomy vest. It's a great item to wear when you need a little warmth but don't want a full sweater. Try wearing it belted or closed with a shawl pin if you don't want it open all the time.

I picked springtime colors for my vest, but choose some of your favorites for a project that's fun to knit and lovely to wear.

Finished Measurements

32 (34, 37.5, 40, 41.5)"/81 (86, 95, 101.5, 105) cm around chest

22.5 (23, 23.5, 24, 24.5)"/ 57.25 (58.75, 59.75, 61.25, 62.25) cm long

To fit a 32 (34, 36, 38, 40)"/ 81.25 (86.5, 91.5, 96.5, 101.5) cm chest, but each size will fit a variety of people.

Yarn

Berroco Vintage, medium weight #4 yarn (52% acrylic, 40% wool, 8% nylon; 218 yd./200 m per 3.5 oz./100 g skein)

- 3 (3, 3, 4, 4) skeins #51103 Clary (Color A)
- 1 skein #5121 Sunny (Color B)

Needles and Other Materials

- US 6 (4 mm) straight or circular needles
- US 7 (4.5 mm) straight or circular needles
- 2 US 7 (4.5 mm) double-pointed needles
- Stitch markers
- Stitch holder or piece of waste yarn

Adjust needle sizes as necessary to obtain gauge.

Gauge

17 sts x 24 rows in St st with larger needles = 4"/10 cm square

Finished Measurements

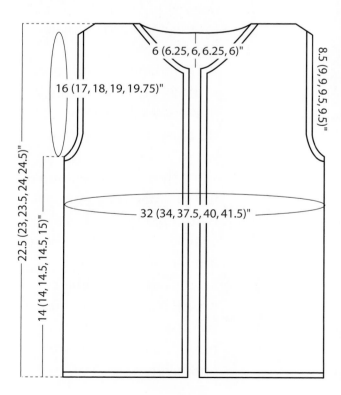

6 (6.25, 6, 6.25, 6)"

8.5 (9, 9, 9.5, 9.5)"

16 (17, 18, 19, 19.75)"

22.5 (23, 23.5, 24, 24.5)"

14 (14, 14.5, 14.5, 15)"

32 (34, 37.5, 40, 41.5)"

Front

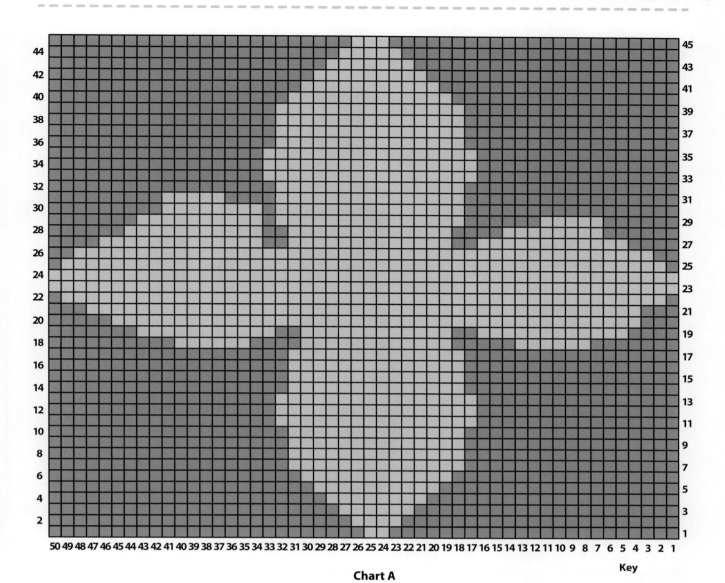

Chart A

Key

■ Color A
□ Color B

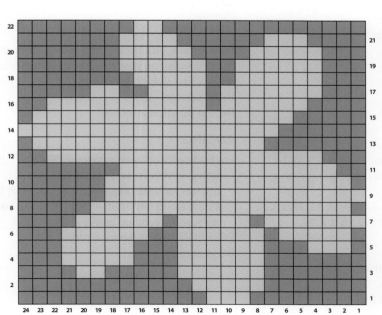

Chart B

Back

Using smaller needles, CO 68 (72, 80, 84, 88) sts.
Work in k2, p2 ribbing for 2"/5 cm.
Change to larger needles and work in St st until
piece measures 6.5 (6.75, 7, 7.25, 7.5)"/16.5
(17.25, 17.75, 18.5, 19) cm. End with a WS row.
Begin Chart A, centering on the back with 9 (11,
15, 17, 19) sts plain on each side (place markers at beginning and end of chart). *At the
same time,* when piece measures 13.5 (13.75,
14, 14.25, 14.5)"/34.25 (35, 35.5, 36.25, 37) cm,
BO 7 sts at beg of next 2 rows to begin the
armhole shaping—54 (58, 66, 70, 74) sts.
When chart is finished, work even until arm-
holes measure 8.5 (9, 9, 9.5, 9.5)"/21.5 (23, 23,
24, 24) cm.
BO 16 (18, 20, 22, 24) sts, place 22 (22, 26, 26, 26)
sts on holder or waste yarn for the neck, join
new yarn and BO 16 (18, 20, 22, 24) sts.

Left Front

Using smaller needles, CO 34 (36, 40, 42, 44) sts.
Work in k2, p2 ribbing for 2"/5 cm.
Change to larger needles and work in St st for
2"/5 cm. End with a WS row.
Work Chart B, centering on the panel with 5 (6,
8, 9, 10) sts plain on each side; place markers
at beginning and end of chart.
Work even until piece measures 13.5 (13.75, 14,
14.25, 14.5)"/34.5 (35, 35.5, 36.25, 37) cm,
ending with a WS row.
BO 7 sts to begin armhole shaping—27 (29, 33, 35, 37) sts.
Work even until armhole measures 2.5 (2.75, 3, 3.25,
3.5)"/6.5 (7, 7.75, 8.25, 9) cm.
Dec row: Work to last 4 sts, k2tog, k2.
Work Dec row each RS row 8 times, then every fourth RS
row 5 times—14 (16, 20, 22, 24) sts.
Work even until armhole measures 8.5 (9, 9, 9.5, 9.5)"/ 21.5
(23, 23, 24, 24) cm.
BO.

Right Front

Work as for left front until piece measures 13.5 (13.75, 14,
14.25, 14.5)"/34.5 (35, 35.5, 36.25, 37) cm, ending with a
RS row.
BO 7 sts to begin armhole shaping—27 (29, 33, 35, 37) sts.
Work even until armhole measures 2.5 (2.75, 3, 3.25,
3.5)"/6.5 (7, 7.75, 8.25, 9) cm.
Dec row: K2, ssk, knit to end.
Work Dec row each WS row 8 times, then every fourth WS
row 5 times—14 (16, 20, 22, 24) sts.
Work even until armhole measures 8.5 (9, 9, 9.5, 9.5)"/ 21.5
(23, 23, 24, 24) cm.
BO.

Finishing

Sew fronts to back using mattress stitch.
Sew shoulder seams.

ARMHOLES

For armhole, pick up and knit evenly around 68 (72, 76, 80,
84) sts, making sure you end up with a multiple of 4.
Work k2, p2 ribbing for 6 rnds.
BO in pattern.
Repeat on other armhole.

EDGING

For body, pick up and knit evenly 69 (73, 77, 81, 83) sts
along right front, knit across 22 (22, 26, 26, 26) held
stitches for back of neck, pick up and knit 69 (73, 77, 81,
83) sts along left front—160 (168, 180, 188, 192) sts, making sure you end up with a multiple of 4.
Work in k2, p2 ribbing for 6 rnds.
BO in pattern.

Techniques

This book assumes you know how to cast on, knit, purl, increase, decrease, and bind off stitches. (If you don't know how to do those things, check out my book *Quick & Easy Baby Knits*, which has all those instructions as well as a bunch of great, easy knitting patterns for babies.)

If some other skill is necessary and it isn't described with the pattern itself, you should find it here.

Cable Knitting

The cable used in the Two-Color Cable Hat is a simple left-slanting cable. The only difference between the cable shown here and the one used in the hat is that this one is worked in a single color. The Gull Stitch used on the Ombre Mitts is worked in the same manner, only with the stitches held to the back.

1. To begin the cable turn, slip 3 sts onto the cable needle and hold it to the front of the work.

2. Knit 3 sts as you normally would.

3. Knit the 3 sts from the cable needle.

The pattern will tell you how often to work the cable and what to do with the other stitches.

Duplicate Stitch

Duplicate stitch is a great way to add an additional color to a knitting project or to hide a mistake you might have made in your colorwork. It is performed with a length of yarn and a yarn needle and, as the name implies, covers up a knit stitch with a stitch of a different color.

1. To get started, bring the yarn to the front of the work from the back in the bottom of the V of the first stitch you want to duplicate.

(continued)

2. Bring the yarn needle behind the legs of the stitch above the stitch you are duplicating and pull through. You'll notice this covers one leg of the V. Make your stitches snug, not so loose that you can see the stitch underneath, nor so tight that the fabric is distorted.

3. To finish the stitch, put the needle down through the fabric in the same place you started—that is, at the bottom of the V of the stitch you're covering.

Repeat as necessary to add the color you want where you want it.

Grafting

Also known as the Kitchener stitch, grafting is a common way to close up the toe of a sock. It's a little fiddly to start, but once you get in the rhythm it can go pretty quickly. Just try to keep your tension even so it looks like you're sewing a row of stitches.

1. First, arrange the live stitches so they are on two double-pointed needles, with the same number of stitches on each needle.

2. Thread your yarn tail onto a yarn needle. Slip the needle through the first stitch on the front needle as if to purl, leaving the stitch on the needle.

3. Slip the needle through the first stitch on the back needle as if to knit, leaving the stitch on the needle.

4. Slip the needle through the first stitch on the front needle as if to knit, pulling it off the needle and pulling the yarn through.

5. Slip the needle through the new first stitch on the front needle as if to purl, leaving it on the needle.

6. Slip the needle through the first stitch on the back needle as if to purl, pulling it off the needle and pulling the yarn through.

7. Slip the needle through the new first stitch on the back needle as if to knit, leaving it on the needle.

8. Repeat steps 4–7 (knit off, purl on, purl off, knit on) until all the stitches have been worked. Bring the needle to the inside of the sock and weave in the end.

Horizontal Seaming

A horizontal seam is needed when sewing the shoulder seams of a sweater. It is similar to mattress stitch in that it, too, makes a seam that is largely invisible from the right side. In this case, you need the same number of stitches on each piece of knitting.

I'm showing this process with swatches of two different colors just so you can see how it goes a little more easily.

1. Set the pieces up so one is above the other on a flat surface. Thread the yarn tail or another length of yarn onto a yarn needle.

2. Slip the needle under the V of the first stitch on the right hand side of the bottom row on the top piece of knitting and pull the yarn through.

3. Slip the needle under the V of the last stitch on the right hand side of the top row on the bottom piece of knitting and pull the yarn through.

(continued)

4. Work a few stitches through each piece and pull the yarn a little tighter to get the pieces to butt up against each other, looking like a seamless piece of knitting.

Mattress Stitch

Mattress stitch is the common term for sewing a vertical seam in knitting. You'll need this skill for all of the intarsia patterns, other than the scarf. It works on any two pieces of knitting that are the same number of rows, or one-piece items with a vertical seam, such as the flat-knit hat, mittens, and socks in this book.

1. Thread your yarn tail or another piece of yarn onto a yarn needle. Look at the column of knitting, and between the first and second stitches you will see a little piece of yarn. Slip the needle behind the yarn ladder on one of the sides of the work or one of the pieces you want to seam together (I usually start on the right, but it doesn't matter) and pull the yarn through.

2. Repeat on the other side.

3. Work the stitch back and forth between the two pieces of knitting for an inch or so, then pull the yarn tighter so that the two pieces snug up together.

4. Continue to the end of the pieces.

Pick Up and Knit Stitches

When you pick up stitches, you are making stitches where there were none before so that you can knit in a different direction from the way you started. This is commonly needed after turning a sock heel, but it's also used in the Color Belt Sweater, where stitches are picked up from the belt to knit the rest of the sweater, and the Bluebird Cowl, where the edging is worked and then stitches are picked up from it to knit the rest of the piece.

3. Pull that loop through to make a new stitch.

1. Stick your needle into the edge (or one stitch in from the edge) of the knit fabric.

2. Place your working yarn over the needle as if you were forming a knit stitch.

4. Continue to pick up as many stitches as called for as evenly as possible across the work. It may be helpful to use stitch markers to visually divide the work into quarters and then make sure you pick up one quarter of your stitches over that space.

When picking up stitches on a heel flap, you can work through the slipped stitches on the edge. Just put your needle under the stitch and form a knit stitch with the working yarn as usual.

Wrap and Turn

When knitting a sock heel that uses short rows, you will see the instruction to wrap and turn on each row. The purpose of this is to eliminate the hole that would otherwise show on the side of the heel where you turned the work before the end of the row.

WRAP AND TURN ON KNIT SIDE

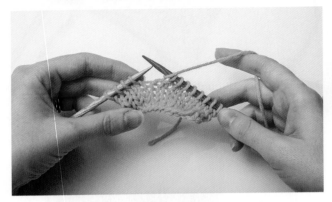

1. To perform a wrap and turn on the right side, knit to where the wrap is supposed to happen. Bring the yarn to the front.

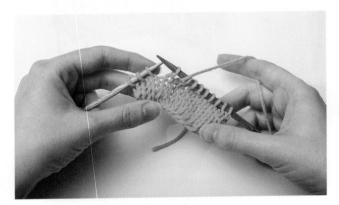

2. Slip the next stitch as if to purl.

3. Bring the yarn to the back.

4. Slip the stitch back onto the left-hand needle and turn the work to begin the next row.

WRAP AND TURN ON PURL SIDE

1. To perform a wrap and turn on the wrong side, purl to where the wrap is supposed to happen. Bring the yarn to the back.

2. Slip the next stitch as if to purl.

3. Bring the yarn to the front.

4. Slip the stitch back onto the left-hand needle and turn the work to begin the next row.

BOTH SIDES—HIDING WRAPS

When you get back to the wrap, knit or purl it together with the stitch it was wrapping. This hides the wrap, making it less visible in the finished project.

Abbreviations

beg	beginning
BO	bind off
CO	cast on
dec	decrease
inc	increase
k	knit
k2tog	knit 2 together
kfb	knit in the front and back
M1	make one
pm	place marker
p	purl
rem	remain/remaining
RS	right side
rnd/rnds	round/rounds
sl	slip
sm	slip marker
ssk	slip slip knit
st/sts	stitch/stiches
WS	wrong side
yo	yarn over

Further Reading/ Bibliography

The following books are great for inspiration and learning more about the color techniques used in this book.

Bernard, Wendy. *Custom Knits.* New York: STC Craft, 2008.
This book has nothing to do with color knitting, but it is the book that taught me how to knit set-in sleeves from the top down, which definitely deserves recognition. If you're ready to take your color knitting skills and use them on other projects, this is a great place to start.

Birek, Laura. *Picture Perfect Knits.* San Francisco: Chronicle Books, 2008.
This is one of very few books available exclusively about intarsia. If this is a technique you find that you really like, you'll want this book for its fun patterns and motif designs you can plug into any project you like.

Epstein, Nicky. *Knitting on the Edge.* New York: Sixth & Spring Books, 2004.
A great edging can make a project that much more fun, and this book has a great collection of ribs, ruffles, lace, fringes, and more to add to projects. The lace edging on the Bluebird Cowl is the Eyelet Points pattern from this book.

Mucklestone, Mary Jane. *150 Scandinavian Motifs: The Knitter's Directory.* Loveland, CO: Interweave Press LLC, 2013.
This book is a great resource for stranded colorwork motifs collected from the traditional knitting of Norway, Sweden, Denmark, Iceland, and the Faroe Islands. The bluebird on the Bluebird Cowl was in part inspired by one of the designs in this book.

———. *200 Fair Isle Motifs: A Knitter's Directory.* Loveland, CO: Interweave Press LLC, 2011.
Another great collection of traditional motifs, this book includes small, relatively simple peerie patterns, larger border patterns, and even larger patterns that can be used as the basis of a stranded knitting design. The book also offers great advice on incorporating these patterns into knitwear designs.

Walker, Barbara. *A Treasury of Knitting Patterns.* Pittsville, WI: Schoolhouse Press, 1998.
If you're looking for basic stitch patterns to try out with self-striping yarn or when making your own stripes, this book has some great, classic stitch patterns. You'll also find some slip-stitch patterns (as well as cables, lace, textured patterns, and much more).

World Textiles: A Sourcebook. Northampton, MA: Interlink Books, 2012.
Sometimes just looking at pictures can be really inspiring, and this book, full of beautiful textiles from around the world, was a great inspiration to me when choosing colors and designs.

Acknowledgments

This is my third knitting book, and while I won't say the process exactly gets easier over time, it is certainly different each time. This time I was lucky enough to have the support of some really good friends, who meet in the woods several times a year to write, create, laugh, and enjoy each other's company. A lot of this book was written with them, and a lot of knitting was done while sitting around talking and laughing until I was hoarse with them. So thank you Eileen, Jacqueline, Paige, Sarah, and Terra for your support, for distracting me when I needed it, and for celebrating with me every step of the way.

Thanks to Nick for putting up with me while I did another one, surely sooner than you would have liked. And to Anna for once again dealing with me knitting a steady stream of things that weren't for you.

Thanks to Kyle and Candi at Stackpole for wanting to do another book with me, helping me refine my vision, and seeing it through to the lovely finished product it has become.

Thanks to Beth Hall and Tiffany Blackstone for your photos, and thanks to the yarn companies who provided such generous and colorful yarn support.

Yarn Sources

Berroco, Inc.
berroco.com

Malabrigo Yarn
malabrigoyarn.com

Blue Moon Fiber Arts, Inc.
bluemoonfiberarts.com

Plymouth Yarn
plymouthyarn.com

Brown Sheep Co.
brownsheep.com

Harrisville Designs
harrisville.com

Cascade Yarns
cascadeyarns.com

Red Heart
redheart.com

Classic Elite Yarns
classiceliteyarns.com

Southwest Trading Co.
swtcyarn.com

Halcyon Yarn
halcyonyarn.com

Spud & Chloë
spudandchloe.com

Knitting Fever (Debbie Bliss, Noro)
knittingfever.com

Valley Yarns
yarn.com

Knit Picks
knitpicks.com

Westminster Fibers (Lopi)
istex.is/english/

Lion Brand Yarn
lionbrandyarn.com

Yarnspirations (Caron)
yarnspirations.com

Visual Index

Super-Bulky Rainbow Scarf
6

Eyelet Beret
9

Mock Cable Gloves
12

Self-Striping Knee Highs
15

Color Belt Sweater
19

Sunburst Horizontal Stripe Scarf
25

Ombre Striped Mitts
28

Welted Stripe Hat
31

Swim Lesson Socks
34

Color-Block Striped Raglan Sweater
37

Brick Stitch Scarf
43

Chain Stripe Hat
45

Lattice Mitts
48

Boxy Stripe Socks
51

Slip-Stitch Tweed Top
54

Bluebirds Cowl
62

Two-Color Cable Hat
66

Checkerboard Mittens
69

Wear Your Heart on Your Socks
72

Diamond Circular Yoke Sweater
75

Superstar Scarf
81

Argyle Style Hat
84

Reindeer Games Mittens
87

Polka Dot Socks
90

Flower Doodle Vest
93